The Quaid Conspiracy

A novel
by
Matt Oberon

~ Also by the author ~
BOOK OF JOSH, 2006 & 2010
THE DEVIL'S GIFTS
in the Andean Cloud Forest of Peru, 2008
TUNE OF THE PIPER, 2009
BLOODLINE, 2011
THE FANTASTICAL REPORTER, 2011
THE BUGLE, 2013

ISBN 978-0-620-50846-9

Mercutio Books
Simon's Town, South Africa
27 21 7861356

Chapter One

After a week of intensive creativity at the Studio, Simon opened the best of Cape wines and relaxed in solitude on the balcony of his lofty rent apartment. He revelled in the view over the tree tops of Central Park and marvelled at the foresight of the city fathers who had not given in to the usual development pressure in the early days of New York. Imagine if the Park had been lost under buildings? But, the promise of being in New York aside, accepting a commission to be the lead architect in a New York project had meant sacrifice, which was not new to Simon. Yet he was always prepared to go out on a limb, push the boundaries or take a leap of faith to get out of the mould.

By day, fifteen hours a day and longer, the Phoenix Acre job challenged and absorbed his attention, and that of the Consortium. There was hardly time for lunch and tea breaks. After a shaky start, where egos were on display, the top trio of the hierarchy was getting along better. It hinged on their different design philosophies. It had been a matter of finding common ground on the aesthetic theme and it was only after Simon's strong stand that a 'green' design ethic became their lodestar. Phoenix Acre would stand out as a role model for other New York structures, and possibly internationally, its innovative design having already been acclaimed by the glossy architectural journals.

For the first time the day before, a scale model showing the architectural character of the building had been presented to the owners, the Zeffler brothers. Their praise was magnanimous: not only did the building satisfy their brief, but it would also save money through innovative energy-saving elements, like the glass of the skin cladding which comprised solar cells capable of powering the heating and cooling the building. Though the cost was higher to install the special glass, over time huge savings would result, a feature which the Zeffler brothers instantly understood – they were after all good businessmen. Standing next to Ground Zero, the perforations in the Defence Wall were glazed in explosion-proof glass, the design, Mondrian-inspired. That would impress their insurance brokers, while ensuring the safety of the occupants in the event of another air strike in the vicinity. The Zefflers went away satisfied clients.

Simon Duval's face had become familiar to most New Yorkers by now, largely due to his ordeal in the Western Sahara at the hands of his abductors. Everywhere he went he was confronted by strangers wanting to shake his hand, or wanting his autograph. That was the way of the Big Apple, where the inhabitants loved to know the rich and famous who were in town and what they were doing in their equally famous city. But, agreeable as New Yorkers could be, the place was a jungle. As the weeks passed Simon felt a constant longing for home, for Ingrid and the twins. It was ironic that one could be lonely in a big city, like the Big Apple with its millions of people, Simon thought. On the other hand, to have ignored Mr Max Zeffler's persuasive offer – the rebuilding of Phoenix Acre, a site adjoining the now world famous Ground Zero – was simply not an option. The building had been flattened during the air strike on the World Trade Centre in 2002. Mr Zeffler, the owner, was an experienced entrepeneur who knew a good architect when he met one, and Simon Duval's success with intenational projects, such as the Friendship Freeport project on the coast of Morocco, had impressed him.

On his return to the Cape after the Moroccan project, Simon had to admit that it's provincial culture had become too limiting for an architect who'd experienced the international milieu. It was like being a big fish in a small pond. Knowing that he couldn't be expected to settle down to suburban life with his young family, Ingrid said she and the twins would manage somehow during his frequent trips to New York. She accepted that Simon's career was his lifeblood, that he needed to commit himself to life in the Big Apple for the duration of the Phoenix Acre job, with only intermediate breaks to share with the family.

With a multi-million real estate business to back him, Mr Max Zeffler's offer to Simon to be the lead architect included a partnership in an established New York office, and he'd accepted without hesitation. All the resources he could wish for would be available to him. And what was more, his importance to the consortium earned him a personal limo with a driver, Larry, an apartment overlooking Central Park and allowances for travel, clothing and entertainment. As he viewed his new high-flying status, he had no delusions – good fortune had smiled on him.

Larry made driving a pleasure around New York city. The archetypal taxi man, like the others he was streetwise and up to date on who of any consequence was in town at that very moment. He recognised Simon from the news stories, and asked endless questions about the episode when he was buried under the sands of the Sahara.

On an anniversary of the destruction of the WTC, The New York Times carried stories and images of the development plans for the both new WTC and Phoenix Acre. It was on a Sunday that Simon chose to visit Ground Zero, where, like hundreds of others paying homage to the victims of the disaster, he viewed the site from the observation platform. The gaping hole where the twin World Trade Centre towers had once stood was a heartrending reminder of those who had lost their lives. The abrupt spatial void in the Manhattan cityscape was a graphic reminder to New Yorkers, and to him, of the emotionally charged images of that extraordinary disaster as it happened. New York was founded on a vast investment of human energy and the reconstruction of the city around Ground Zero would depend on the emotional resilience of the New Yorkers and their commitment to the challenge.

The master plan for the new WTC was on display. Simon felt ambivalent about the soaring glass Freedom Tower peaking at a height of over half a kilometre – instead of becoming a symbol of national healing, it could present to the world a provocative statement inviting yet another the strike, like that of 9/11. With the Transit Hub, the Memorial on the footprint of the former towers, Number Seven World Trade Centre of fifty-two storeys, and three additional office towers, reconstruction was a mammoth undertaking, against a background of furious politicking and public controversy.

He ambled down the public boardwalk to touch the Slurry Wall, a seven-storey retaining wall which still stood firm after 9/11. Had it not held back the Hudson river during the collapse of the towers, the New York underground would have been flooded. He recalled with a shiver the Thames river flooding of the basement of the Earth Museum in London, where his own tenuous chances of survival had been tested. He left the site in a sombre mood.

Larry was waiting for him at the entrance with the car.

'Cheer me up, Larry,' Simon said taking the back seat and fastening his seat belt.

'Well, you could do worse than to go up the Empire State...shall I take you there?'

Simon felt his mood lighten. New Yorkers were punting the Empire State as "New York's Lighthouse", "New York City's Prized Prop" and as the "Symbol of New York City". When it was built and completed in thirteen months, the skyscraper had become famous and was the only building in town after the Depression, which ended the building frenzy of the 1920s. Its assertive towering presence over the skyline of New York restored people's confidence at the time, no wonder its fame had endured as the darling of the New Yorkers. Its aesthetic was plain, but the sheer fenestrated facades and stepped tapering mass culminated pleasingly in the landmark spire topped with a tall mast. It was once the tallest building in the world and it still evoked the aspirations of the past, a time when zeppelins, or dirigibles might have docked onto its pinnacle – the dream of transcontinental air travel of yesteryear, halted by the Hindenburg disaster. Architecturally it spelt stability and robustness, characteristics which any investor would normally admire – but in fact it was a business disaster.

Simon took the staged elevator system and emerged at the top viewing gallery. The famous view before him was one of life's great vistas. Other skyscrapers rose like stalagmites out of the tight city fabric. Below, Broadway cut a determined swathe across the rigid street matrix.

Simon sighed as he thought about the Phoenix Acre project. Although his designs had received recognition and acclaim elsewhere, the Phoenix Acre project would severely challenge his international fame as an architect. The awe–inspiring exhibition of the human enterprise and brilliance across downtown New York had evolved over generations in a culture which was foreign to him. It was in that most famous world city context, he had been commissioned to supplant a landmark building, yet he had no idea what New Yorkers wanted. How would he shape up against the icons of the Manhattan landscape? The prospect was humbling.

Back at his penthouse suite, the phone on the inside table rang.

'Hello is that Simon Duval?' asked the female voice on the line.

'Yes?' said Simon curiously, not expecting a call.

'You know Max – he's my father,' said the voice in a nasal New York accent. 'I am his daughter, Maxine. We wondered if you would like to join us for dinner this coming Saturday?'

He'd been wondering how he would be spending another weekend alone in this vast city.

'I'd love to come. Thank you,' he said, almost too gratefully.

'Well then, we live on upper East Side, right near the Guggenheim. We have the penthouse.' Maxine described the address. 'Dress is formal.' she said. 'In New York that means black tie. I just thought I'd mention that since you are from Africa, and things could be different there.'

'Got it,' rejoined Simon.

'We are really looking forward to meeting you, Simon. My friends have been on to me to invite you. Did you know your picture has appeared twice in the newspapers? Oh, and congratulations on your wonderful buildings. By the way you will be meeting some displaced royals from old Europe, and a few New York architects.'

'That will be grand,' said Simon, amused by the odd snippets of information which keep flowing from the voice.

'See you then, about eight-thirty? Oh, and don't plan to leave early. New Yorkers sometimes leave at dawn!'

In the meantime there was work to do. The consortium for Phoenix Acre was large, and there were other architects in the team all of whom examined critically every idea or notion that Simon presented as a serious design idea. Women architects particularly were inclined to be feisty and difficult, as they often believed there was an imaginary glass ceiling to their progress, or suspicious of being patronised. *So, tread carefully, Duval,* Simon advised himself.

The predilection for glass curtain walls had got stuck in the New York psyche, Simon noted. It was almost an established custom in North America, but, coming from Africa, for him it was anathema. The new Freedom Tower on the WTC site was to have 'ultra-clear' glazing without clarity on how the solar gain would be dealt with. *With the global energy crisis looming, how can architects not feel accountable for their energy-guzzling buildings?* he questioned. The difference between the First and Third World mindset began to show and rankle with him. Debates around green issues always ended up with team differences over the high cost of alternative, otherwise known as 'green', technologies.

The modest and less vulnerable design for Phoenix Acre with its robust building mass that the trio finally settled on constrasted with the soaring skyscraper of the new Freedom Tower. In fact a defence wall against any knock-on effect from the collapse of any adjoining building on the WTC site was integral to their design. Personality differences could lead to clashes, and he was well aware of that. The model and 3D graphics departments were in continual production assembling three-dimensional visualisation. As expected there were regular arguments and debates around the aesthetic, even after hours over mobile telephones. Happily, the American development style was not to start construction until the architect and engineers had completed their work. Once the construction started it would be fast-tracked until completion, so that a new building could be seen to rise almost before one's eyes. That method of building suited Simon as he would be released from the project during the construction phase, when his work was really over, and he could go home.

The Zefflers knew precisely what economic return they wanted from their Phoenix Acre building, and kept a constant presence. As clients, their interest in the project from the start never flagged. Ironically, despite the tragic events of 9/11, being a building right next to the new development on the famous Ground Zero site was seen as a boost to rentals – *the real estate world was indeed confusing,* mused Simon.

On the night of the dinner party, Simon was dropped off by his driver, Larry, at Maxine Zeffler's apartment building around the appointed time. He told Larry that he would find his own way home. To pass through security in the entrance lobby normally involved some form of identification, but Maxine had advised the desk about who should be allowed to take the lift to her penthouse apartment and he was shown to the elevator.

The Zeffler brothers were sons of immigrants from Eastern Europe who had arrived at Ellis Island like the many thousands who followed the American rainbow before and after World War I. They had worked their way up through sheer hard work and business savvy to become real estate barons in the Big Apple. In fact the events of 9/11 favoured their real estate options: the old Phoenix Acre had become inefficient and difficult to lease to top grade tenants. They were a huge bonded family, the Zefflers, and their offspring – Maxine, one of four – were already adults by the time that Simon arrived in New York.

Simon rang the bell and Maxine's butler opened the door to him, formally requesting his name. He was ushered him into a spacious hall, which belonged more in a mansion in New Orleans than in a New York apartment. A skylight provided a soft light onto the curved white marble staircase which split into two at the first landing. To the right and left there were ceiling-high double doors, closed at that moment. The butler led Simon to the one on the left, which he threw open with familiarity, then announced: 'Mr Simon Duval,' to the standing guests.

A woman in her early thirties came forward: 'Simon, my pleasure, I'm Maxine. Thank you for coming. I hope you found the building without difficulty?' He nodded his appreciation.

He was led by the hand by Maxine to the centre of the room where guests stood conversing in a circle. His guessed that, with a few exceptions, they were all about in their late thirties, and accustomed to anything that money can buy. They received him with a friendly greeting, then he was ushered to the side bar where a couple stopped their conversation as he joined them.

'We have followed your astonishing career with some interest,' greeted the tall balding man.

'Thank you very much,' Simon replied, 'I am not sure how that is possible, as this is my first time in New York.'

'Oh,' joined in his attractive lady companion, 'your building in London is beautiful, and what you managed to do for Morocco has been in the international papers. Don't be so modest, Mr Simon Duval!'

Maxine announced dinner would be served. The guests were ushered across the hall to the double doors across the spacious hall, which was opened by the butler with noticable ceremony. Simon drew in his breath at the spectacle, but the other guests appeared unmoved by the lavish table setting before them – presumably they were accustomed to the sight of such excess. The high polish of the table reflected the centrepieces of candelabras and low bowls of flowers. Place names for each guest had been especially printed for the occasion in gold on white card. Simon was seated next to Maxine, and the other guests found their own places without a second bidding.

As the buzz resumed around the table, and the butler served the soup, Simon thought about Ingrid with the twins back home, regretting that she was not with him to observe lavishness and idiosyncrasies of New York high society.

Imported wine was poured into large crystal goblets, then followed a four course meal starting with cold gazpacha soup, after which came a Canadian salmon mousse, then a choice of either Moroccan tajine or Montana roast duck with orange sauce, and ending with a dessert of baked pears soaked in red wine and topped with imported Italian gelati.

Once the dessert plates had been cleared, a trolley with ten varieties of cheese was wheeled around, and exotic out-of-season fruits were offered. The banter round-the-table had risen to a sustained crescendo.

Simon quietly surveyed the guests around the table and noticed with some surprise that Catherine Quaid was also there, sitting opposite at some distance. He had missed noticing her when he arrived. She seemed confidentially engaged in conversation with a tall man who had been introduced to him as Pierre. They often looked his way, but as though he was not present at all. Other female as well as male eyes occasionally fixed on him in the eye game. Simon was old and wise enough to get the message – he was being propositioned for who knows what? *Extraordinary were the rewards of celebrity*, he thought cynically.

Conversation at the table was mostly inconsequential – *these people don't have to prove themselves*, Simon figured, *their private incomes were probably more than that of a small country.* The party started to get into a roller coaster mood, with irrational and slurred comments peppering the exchanges across the table.

Maxine seemed to read the mood of her guests well and dismissed the staff. She invited the guests to help themselves to coffee at the enormous ornate walnut sideboard.

'Did you notice, Simon?' she said out loud, 'the chef produced a Moroccan tajine especially to welcome you?'

'Yes, indeed,' Simon replied, sounding appreciative.

'Now, we are all dying to know about your misadventure in Morocco. Did you abductors ever get caught? What was it like to be buried? Do tell us, and don't leave out a thing!' Some of the guests banged the table with whatever they could find and others looked towards him with hazy anticipation.

He related the story, constantly being interrupted with questions, sometimes sober ones sometimes not. The abductors had been charged and gaoled after he had left Morocco, he told them. The smell of an unfamiliar aroma wafted passed his nostrils. He was soon enlightened: the guests almost to the last were partaking of an after-dinner joint of cannabis. Maxine did not indulge nor he noted, did Catherine, but instead they seemed totally at peace with the conduct of the others around the table. Some guests were rising unsteadily from the table and withdrawing from the room – where to, Simon hesitated to guess. Tactfully, Maxine suggested they all return to the drawing room.

As he rose from the table, Simon felt a tap on his shoulder.

'Simon, old man,' said the man, whose name was Pierre, straining to appear stable, 'here is my card. I would love you to come to a mask party in two weeks time at our apartment.'

During the entire evening Pierre had been attentive towards Catherine. They seemed to be close friends. Remembering his history with Catherine, Simon hesitated briefly, but then accepted: 'Well, thank you, Pierre, I shall do my best to be there.'

'Splendid.' Pierre, making his way unsteadily to the door.

With her usual charm Catherine busied herself saying good night to old friends. She then turned to Simon.

'Well isn't this a small world, Simon. Fancy seeing you here in New York and such a long way from your little old hometown in the Cape.' She spelt it out loud enough so the remaining guests would hear.

'How did you get here – taxi? Oh dear,' she scoffed, not waiting for his reply, 'my chauffeur will have the car ready,

I can offer you a lift to your singles pad – I am right aren't I, you are living alone here in New York?'

Simon felt cornered. If he refused the offer and the hall porter had to call a taxi for him she would regard that as a slight. He knew enough already to write a book about this lady's avenging ways.

'Yes, thanks, that would be much appreciated,' he said formally.

Simon relieved the butler of Catherine's coat of real Arctic fox fur, and placed it over her shoulders. *In heaven's name, spoilt Ms Quaid, have you no environmental sensitivity?* he growled beneath his breath, thinking about "beauty without cruelty". He was beginning to regret accepting her offer of a lift.

In the white Mercedes limo Catherine was charm itself. As the chauffeur negotiated the busy streets of the Big Apple, Simon looked at his watch in the lights from the street. It was the early hours of the morning but it seemed the city did not sleep, but just kept buzzing with nightlife until with a yawn it would start all over again when the sun rose in a few hours.

The chauffeur, Rory, stopped at a tall apartment buildig with the typical entrance canopy of upmarket New York buildings and looked in the rear view mirror as if waiting for instructions. Catherine invited Simon to her apartment for a quick coffee or whatever took his fancy. He knew she would.

'The night is still young, Simon,' she said using the old well-worn expression.

Stepping onto the pavement Simon glanced up briefly at the building before they entered through the polished brass entrance doors. After a quick greeting to the concierge, Catherine showed the way to the pink mirrored glass elevator. She pressed the penthouse button where they arrive within seconds. The lift doors opened directly into lobby of a private apartment.

The interior décor was neo-classical with columns and pediments over each door. Floor to ceiling windows with coloured glass insets were draped in heavy brocade. The door to the left led into the sitting room where a gas fire was burning in the hearth. With it, the huge overhanging mantelshelf above head height, supported by sculpted figures seemed incongruously out of scale. The entire room oozed with excessive wealth.

'Never mind the décor, Simon,' Catherine said reading his mind, 'this is my father's apartment and not my taste at all. I want to show you my latest acquisition. It is a John Dane sculpture which I bought from a dealer, a dear old friend, who always let's me know when interesting work comes up for sale.'

She ushered him into another room, but on the way they passed her father's collection of Italian Renaissance masters. An exquisite Canaletto painting of the Grand Canal caught his eye. Simon imagined the painting on the wall in his own study, and could visualise the exact spot. *Wow, now that would be worth going to gaol for.* The thought of owning it was too beguiling to dismiss.

Catherine left Simon to view her new acquisition, the John Dane, saying that she wanted to change into something more comfortable. Mrs Winslow the housekeeper, she said, would soon be bringing the coffee.

Simon returned to the sofa near the fireplace. The Dane sculpture had not impressed him. It seemed to be pure comic book, all in one colour, offering no challenge to the intellect, although Simon conceded, perhaps he was being too plebeian. What New Yorkers considered 'in', could turn anything into a fashion statement overnight, then push the price up so that only the rich were able to afford it.

Mrs Winslow pushed a trolley through the huge doorway and greeted him very courteously, but not inviting conversation. She started to leave without another word.

At that moment Catherine returned, saying to her: 'Thank you Mrs Winslow, that will be all. I've asked Rory to take you home in the car. Good night.' *Well*, thought Simon, *that was how to run a slick domestic machine untouched by the human heart.*

He looked at Catherine in her transformed state. She had let down her hair, which had grown longer since he first met her, and her green eyes shone reflecting the dancing flames of the faux fire in the hearth. She had put on a loose casual cat suit in pale beige and soft lounge slippers. In fact she looked quite human, almost feminine, *almost like someone you want to get to know*, thought Simon. He quickly checked himself and pushed the thought from his mind - *the Velvet Club.*

They chatted about this and that over coffee and liqueurs, but rather more like two sparring cockrels than two people who shared the same profession. Suddenly, she sat up and said:

'You know, Simon, perhaps we got off on the wrong foot to start with. My biological mother died when I was ten and from then onward, apart from remote aunts, I was brought up mostly in an all male world. Until he married again, Daddy schooled me for whatever life had to throw at me. Possibly, I have been too defensive and denied myself the pleasure of intimate friendships, even with my peers.' At that point she leant over, drawing out an album from a row of books on the side table. She moved to where he was seated, and opened the album.

'Let me break the ice by showing you my favourite album of photos, cuttings and some of the buildings I have designed. I am sure you have something similar.'

'Actually, no, but then I always thought that albums were a girl thing – maybe not, after all,' offered Simon attempting to add to the conversation.

There was no doubt that Catherine was talented, in more ways than one. Simon felt almost forgiving, knowing that she had lost her mother at such an early age. He relaxed into a mood of contentment just listening to her story until she reached the end, closed the album, looked at him while moving closer.

'Simon, darling,' she said theatrically while putting her hand on his knee, 'why don't we become a couple¼ ?' In the brief silence which followed, she realised she had gone too far, '¼ I mean professionally, of course!'

There was a pregnant silence. *Good try, Catherine, and even better cover-up*, thought Simon, but he said:

'Catherine, you know I really do admire your work, and your amazing ability to adapt to trends. You will make it to the very top, mark my words.' As he spoke he knew that his response was inadequate, so he continued: 'And, your sophistication gives you a considerable headstart over your peers. I think you are a most attractive woman, and one day, somewhere, someone is going to fall head over heels in love with you.'

'But?' she enquired.

'But, there is no way that we can join forces in any sense of the word. We are very different people in professional life and otherwise. Let's just say we understand each other better than most.'

She hesitated briefly, digesting his words. 'Let me run you home,' she said in an attempt to regain the high ground. She was ice cold again, the old Catherine. *The war's not over,* Simon realised, *my clumsy diplomacy has had the opposite effect – I must be losing my grip!"*

She phoned Rory on the intercom to bring her maroon Porsche to the entrance.

They sat silently as Catherine accelerated the car through the wet rainy streets of New York. She stopped under the awning of the entrance to his apartment block, looked at him and offered her hand. It felt cold and was quickly withdrawn from his warm response. She stared ahead, her eyes picking up the pulsating red light of the neon sign across the street which gave her a demonic appearance. He noticed she was wearing black velvet driving gloves, monogrammed 'CQ' in gold. He remembered seeing the glove motif on her Cathedral entry – she was creating a brand icon for herself.

She looked again at him: 'I wish you a very good night.' she said without expression, but continued patronisingly, 'Being from a little known city at the foot of Africa, let me warn you, Simon, New York is a jungle. Go back to home and be with your family.'

Simon stood on the pavement watching the maroon Porsche disappear into the kaleidoscope of lights reflected on the wet street. Columns of steam rose ghostlike from the street gratings and a cold reality struck him, that with Catherine Quaid he was riding for a fall.

It took Simon hours to finally get to bed and to slip in and out of sleep. After the unfortunate parry with Catherine the old battle wounds which hadn't healed preyed on his mind. Her sinister and progressive undermining of his professional life was spilling over and disturbing his personal equilibrium. She had propositioned him, and he was certain that his rejection would drive her to further efforts towards revenge, probably covertly as she had in the past. That was her style, and her father, Ambassador Quaid, would be the front behind which she would conceal her evil intentions. Catherine Quaid had been schooled in the merciless ways of New York society. Her prophetic words to Simon: "…let me warn you, Simon, New York is a jungle. Go back to home and be with your family", was precisely what he should not ignore.

In his preoccupation with the demands of the Phoenix Acre project, Simon had forgotten about the mask party to which he had been invited on the coming Saturday. The man Pierre had not, and phoned to remind him. The dress was to be casual, and only a mask was necessary, he told Simon. On the day itself, Simon actually looked forward to a change of routine, and a night on the town. The prospect of partying with a whole number of unknowns also had its appeal – in a curious way.

Following Pierre's directions, Larry drove him to an apartment block on the Hudson river. It was a recycled warehouse structure with a goods lift to Pierre's penthouse, with a commanding view looked out over the rooftops towards the shores of New Jersey opposite.

A stranger to Simon opened the apartment door and without hesitation ushered him into to a huge double volume of space, with the synthetic strains of Garbarek discernible in the background. The occupants, all wearing masks, ceased their chatter, and stared enquiringly at Simon. Pierre came forward and welcomed him with a limp handshake. With a sweep of the other hand, he introduced him to his guests.

'Hullo', said Simon nodding cordially. A few acknowledged his greeting, but others hardly seem to register. Pierre took Simon's coat and suggested he don his mask, the one in plain black satin he had bought, compliments of Mr Chu in Chinatown.

To ease his awkwardness, Simon made his way to the bar. There were men and women standing around in various attire. He looked down at his own clothing and regretted that he stood out as being ultra-conservative.

A tall overly made-up woman at the bar engaged him in conversation: 'I believe I have seen your handsome face before? The architect from Africa – let me think, oh yes, Morocco, Morocco. You were abducted by some Arabs and buried – poor darling!'

Simon acknowledged that it was he. She moved on, obviously drawn to a group nearby discussing something of greater interest. Other people came and went, seeking idle chatter or out of curiosity. His story in the media could explain why there was a great deal of interest in him personally, but conversation never reached beyond first base. After some months living as a New Yorker, he realised that the privileged class have a very short attention span and very narrow interests.

The music moved into rhythmic mode, and couples began to dance. The noise level rose as they talked above the strident disco music emanating from the pumped up stereo speakers. The DJ obviously had a good sense of the mood of the party.

The tall made-up woman suggested they dance. By this time Simon had begun to feel the effects of his first few drinks, and was feeling a rather unsteady on his feet. The woman, who called herself Carla, was unphased by his awkwardness and took the lead, steering their course through the gyrating crowd. All seemed to go normally until he felt her groping through his pants. *Oh, oh, this is getting interesting,* thought Simon sportingly. The music changed, and Carla kissed him on the lips, suddenly turning away and disappearing amongst the smooching couples.

Simon nursed another drink, poured for him by the bar tender. He looked at the moving mass of dancers detachedly. *There is something about this crowd I can't quite fathom,* he admitted to himself, *but what the hell.* He sat down next to a man who introduced himself as Sven, a Scandinavian, tall and blonde. Simon liked his affability, and didn't mind when his felt a hand on his knee.

The hour was late. Through the haze which had crept over his mind like a morning fog from the ocean, Simon found himself back on the dance floor in a close embrace. Sven was dancing with him cheek to cheek, and all the couples had by that time stripped down, including himself, and were dancing bare-chested. *Everyone here is male,* he concluded, *and the women all transvestites!*

Feeling particularly grim and unsteady on his feet for some unexplained reason, Simon pushed himself away, but Sven pulled him close again and kissed him firmly and passionately on the mouth. A flash picture of Ingrid and the twins crossed Simon's mind. *Let me get out of here,* he decided, forcing himself away. He made an unsteady escape to the exit, but returned for his discarded shirt and coat just as, with a loud crash, the door opened and a large contingent of the New York Police Department burst in.

'Turn off the music and stay where you are!' ordered the police officer. 'This is a drug bust. No one is to move.' Simon sobered briefly, but was unusually disoriented. He felt especially awkward with his torso bare and with his coat and shirt slung over his shoulder. Being nearest the door he was led out first to the waiting lift, then into the police van with ten others from the party. Pierre was amongst them but he studiously avoided Simon's questioning gaze.

For the following two days, the New York papers carried stories of the drug bust at Pierre's apartment. The names of all those who had been taken in for questioning were now in print, including that of Simon Duval, the architect from Africa. Of course, due to his notoriety, the media made a big thing of his involvement. His misfortune was that he was being charged as a pusher - the drug squad found a sizable supply of cocaine and heroine in his coat pockets which Pierre had so politely offered to take when he arrived at the party. His coat pockets had been used by the hosts as a depot for the drugs, from where the partygoers could help themselves. He was the fall guy. Worse still, he had unknowingly accepted a spiked drink with a chemical substance which had shown up in his blood tests. This would explain the confused state he was experiencing during the party.

Simon was indicted and kept in jail. He could be facing a stiff sentence for substance abuse and drug peddling.

As with all persons charged with a crime, Simon was allowed one phone call, local or international. Ingrid was on his mind all the time and he chose to phone home - he had to forestall any misinformation that might reach her ears before he had spoken to her himself. It was the last call he could make, but he failed to speak to Ingrid before he collapsed into a mysterious world where reality could only be reached along a long winding road to a place called Sanity.

Hospitalised, the Zeffler brothers visited Simon every day, but he failed to recognise them. 'In a patient who is prone,' explained the specialist physician, 'the condition can be brought on by an excessive dose of drugs.' In Simon's case excessive levels of the drug called Ecstasy had been found in his blood stream. The only treatment was hospitalisation under supervision and medication to correct the chemical imbalances in his system.

Until his bail hearing came up Simon remained an inmate in a private clinic where he was on a mental roller-coaster.

With the help of the Zefflers he was repatriated to his own country for treatment His contract with the Phoenix Acres project was put on hold pending his recovery.

***

Chapter Two

Ten years earlier

Simon Duval, the person and the architect, was generally well-liked. It was hard to understand why he should ever attract the vitriole of others. With his natural charisma he was the archetypal Leo, generous and warmhearted, creative and enthusiastic, broadminded and expansive, and faithful (sometimes) and loving. On the dark side his only offence was that he could be moody. But, when the lights went up in the town, he came alive and wanted company. His string of girlfriends, usually those who liked a good time, considered him 'the eligible bachelor'. Or, he thought wryly, maybe it was his nut brown two-door Lancia which they all adored?

In any event, at mid-thirty it was time for him to take stock and make some changes – to lifestyle, to being single, to his career. He thought he'd give it another year or two before committing himself.

After a restless night, figuring a way around the problems on the Atlas Tower, Simon took a hot shower then, with a hand towel, wiped the steamed-up mirror. He looked disapprovingly at his reflection, and pondered the future. The purr of the electric razor had a soothing effect as he regarded his features through his half-closed amber eyes. He'd had enough of late nights, but then he had said that to himself before – hadn't he? He remembered the curious dream, almost a foreboding, he'd had last night. He wondered what its subliminal message could have been.

At the building site of the Atlas Tower he went straight to the foreman's office, picked out his hard hat from the array and enquired after George the foreman's whereabouts – knowing George, he was probably at the top on the moving platform now thirty-six storeys up, supervising the concrete lift. Ladders placed between temporary stagings at the various levels were the only way to reach the top platform, or an unnerving ride in the concrete hoist. Simon took to the ladders and groped each ladder rung cautiously – coping with heights was never his strong suite.

George went straight to the cause of another problem, which was worsening as they spoke. 'The levels show the elevator core is going skew', he shouted above the roar of the concrete pour, 'and you know what that means – either we have to stop the slide altogether or carry on and have the whole core out of line from thirty-four storeys upwards – you're the architect, what should we do?'

Looking down from the upwardly moving platform, people below became ant-like, creatures scurrying off about their business, the cars in miniature like a child's toys. But there were more important things to think about – the platform was veering off course, worsening by the minute. Something drastic had to be done, and bound to carry huge cost implications. There was simply no alternative.

'You stop the slide,' Simon shouted to George above the roar.

'I thought you'd say that,' nodded George in agreement.

A few days later, in the Atlas Company's boardroom, Simon waited for the special meeting with the directors to start. For the firt time he took a closer look at the boardroom. The décor was outdated, the walls dark with stained panelling against which were aging photographs of the Atlas Company hierarchy past and present hung in a single row. Unlikely, he sniffed, that a portrait of anyone from the outer circle of this Company will ever hang on those walls. He shuffled through the sheaf of papers from the contractors, just delivered to him. Because of the stoppage they had itemised everything and claiming every last cent. To reset the hydraulics of the lift, an engineer had been flown in from Scotland, but the amount claimed was way out of line.

Like robotic figures, the directors entered the room and took their usual positions around the table. After so many meetings around this table, he could place a bet as to where each one would sit, as if each had worn in their own shape into a specific seat. Their expressionless faces gave nothing away, not even an acknowledgement of Simon's presence. It was a family business, and the founder's son, the chief executive, went unsmilingly to the top of the table. He occupied the chairman's seat, raised higher at the back than the others and, Simon noted with some amusement, on a platform to make up for his shortness of physical stature.

In an atmosphere, which was decidedly cool, Simon explained in great detail the circumstances that gave rise to his instruction to halt the core platform. His justification was received stoically, and there was no discussion nor endorsement for his decision, instead a hail of snide comments. Extra finance for the project had to be found, and they were not amused. It all amounted to money, money and more about money, despite the added value to the Atlas Company's image from Simon's iconic design. Their nitpicking and complaining rang uncomfortably in his ears. It was then that he decided to escape the corporate stuffiness of the Atlas Company and become his own boss.

He bided his time but his eventual departure from the Company was acrimonious to say the least. The board had not reckoned on losing his services and were unexpectedly facing the reality of finding a replacement halfway through the project. Predictably, in the last days, the chief, with swarmy flattery, dealt with Simon's resignation as though it could be reversed.

'We have had our differences, Simon, but you are one of our best people, and we would be sorry if you went through with your resignation. Think about the completion of such a major project and how it will boost your professional image. No one knows more about it than you do. We can offer you more if you feel you services are not being adequately remunerated. Come now, let's forget this little hiccup and get back on the job.'

'I regret, sir, that I have made my decision. There is no place for me as the architect here to make decisions on behalf of the Company without continual interventions by your Board...'

'I was coming to that, Simon. Perhaps you will reconsider once you know that an American real estate development company has bought shares in Atlas and we shall be making an announcement within days. You will head the architectural team, and be given more shares in the new partnership.'

Simon's decision to leave behind the wheeling and dealing of the corporate culture was final. The prospect of an American partnership held no appeal, and changed nothing. His only regret was leaving behind some fringe benefits, like the secretarial pool provided by the Atlas Company – that was going to be a sacrifice. There had been problems when, after dating him, two of them compared notes. It led to all sorts of unwanted tensions back at the workplace. Still, as a consolation, at the office send-off party the secretaries' parting gift to him was a personal diary tied with a bow, with each one's contact details neatly inscribed inside, just in case.

He left the Company building for the last time and felt freer than he had for a long time, as though finally a troublesome load had been lifted from his shoulders.

*

Andreos Aristophanes Nikolaides, Simon's lifelong friend, as known to all as Nick. Simon was orphaned at a young age and Nick's Greek family fostered him through his growing up years. In their youth, Simon and Nick shared many exploits, sometimes verging on the positively dangerous. Getting in and out of trouble schooled and equipped them for later life. The world around them was their playground, and their exploits during after school hours occupied them until the sun went down. These experiences and many others bonded them as friends and were amongst their most vivid memories.

In their late teens they had done their apprenticeship with the opposite sex in the back row of the local movie house at Saturday matinees. Now in their mid-thirties, the noose had tightened for Nick – he was to marry a Greek girl, Estrella. Simon was to be best man at his wedding. The wedding rituals were planned to be as was expected in the Greek tradition – starting with formality and ending in a lively celebration full of colour.

They were to be married in the orthodox Greek church, set high up on the slopes overlooking the city. Nick's mother, the driving force behind the wedding arrangements, worried terribly about the details. She was determined that everything would be exactly as she would have it. Nick's father came from a large family of nine children and emigrated to the New World where, he reported to his family, there were jobs to be had and opportunities more plentiful than in their own country.

The Nikolaides conservatism hadn't stopped Nick from being the lad about town, and with Simon every bar and nightclub in the city had been explored. His dyslexia had only showed up in high school, where scholastically his grades were borderline, but that hadn't stopped him from making a success of his natural skills for business. He grew up streetwise and a people-person, as the saying goes, and he was much sought after socially. His uncanny ability to bend any system to his own advantage, whether it was persuading the bank to give him a substantial loan without co-lateral security, or persuading the traffic department to drop the parking fines he constantly incurred, or negotiating for a discount which would elude most others, he usually came out on top. Nick drifted into the building trade and was involved with contracts in the more affluent quarters of the city. He was considered to be well-off financially.

Nick's mother worried that his last night of bachelorhood would become riotous and he would be late, or not arrive at all, for his own wedding. What a scandal that would be in the Greek community! She was aware of what could happen to the groom during the euphemistically termed "rite of passage". Simon was therefore charged with taking care of the groom with his life.

The day dawned bright and clear heralding good fortune for a marriage destined to be a happy one. Despite all the parental worries, the groom and best man escaped the worst effects of hangovers, more by good luck than by good management. With ample time to spare, they occupied their seats in front row of the church while the organ wheezed out Greek Orthodox pieces, all familiar to Simon. He cast his architect's eye over the white ceiling which sprang seamlessly from the walls to form a plain barrel-vault over the main body of the church. The small window apertures were lined with sandstone and glazed with plain glass, modelled typically on the chapels he had seen on the Greek islands. With not one of the windows open and with the congregation already seated for a half an hour, the interior was becoming decidedly stuffy. Adding to the stuffiness were the lighted candles everywhere and incense. A distraction, at least, was the huge floral displays and the elaborate chancel with its rich ecclesiastical embellishment, mostly in gold and blue.

With Nick looking nervous, Simon attempted to divert his attention: 'Care for a beer?'

'Good timing, pal.'

'Brides are always late, we could nip out through the side door and be back in time," said Simon unconvincingly.

Estrella and her father stood at the entrance to the church for a good five minutes before proceeding towards the chancel. She looked a picture in her designer dress, and the bridesmaids flushed at the prospect of their own weddings another day.

The church service was long and elaborate and when finally over, the congregation poured out into the sunshine to greet the bride and groom, the new Mr and Mrs Nikolaides. Nick's sister, Maria, the plainest and rather overweight, was like the sister that Simon never had. Aided and abetted by her mother, she made Simon feel that he was being handpicked for matrimony, a prospect which put him on his guard and drew him further away. Nick's mother constantly goaded Simon into believing that Greek girls made the best wives. Her usual opening was, 'When are you going to get married, Simon?' whereupon he would usually retort, 'Not until I can afford to, Mrs Nikolaides.'

'And when will that be Simon?'

'When I win the lottery,' he would say impishly, to which she would throw her eyes to the ceiling, and walk away shaking her head resignedly. She saw his potential as a son-in-law, but could never bring herself to disclose her innermost wishes that he should marry her daughter. Somehow Simon's humour was never understood by Mrs Nikolaides as a subtle message that he had no plans to fall in with her matchmaking plans. *The older branch of the Velvet Club*, he often mused.

At the reception Simon lifted the mike to commence his speech. He dispatched the usual wedding formalities as quickly as possible, showing considerable practice in the role of best man. He clutched a bunch of messages sent by absent friends and family, and announced: 'It is now my duty as best man to read out the messages sent to the young couple.'

Messages from the Nikolaides' families and friends in Greece took nearly twenty minutes to read. Then, he said, looking with a smirk at Nick,

'This one is for you, Nick: "Darling, what should I do with the key? Love Fifi."'

Pandemonium broke out from the ranks of the singles club and Nick wagged a warning finger at Simon.

The groom in turn was lavish in his praise for his parents and future in-laws and then, with a surprise ending gave a big thankyou to each of the mothers of his past girlfriends, many of whom were invited guests:

'Thank you all for telling your daughters that I was a no-good, and not allowing any one of them to marry me. I might not have been sitting beside my beautiful bride today!' Estrella flushed with embarrassment at the hooting and cheering of his bachelor friends.

As fortune would have it Simon caught the garter and Nick's plump sister, Maria, the bouquet. Despite the hoots, clapping and cheering, for Simon *that marriage was not going to happen.*

The reception stretched into the early hours until the floor was too cluttered with broken dinner plates for dancing – throwing dinner plates, traditionally in the spirit of the Greek celebrations left a mountain of debris for the cleaners. Orchestrated by Simon, the guests began to gather at the exit to give the bridal couple a royal send-off. With ribbons and tins flying along after the car, and the racket of stones in the hubcaps, Nick and Estrella drove off.

Simon's last words to Nick were: 'I've got a big project for you to look at when you get tired of your wife.'

Estrella understood the bond they shared and just smiled.

There seemed to be so many avenues Simon could follow, but his heart and passion lay in the field for which he had been trained – architecture. He needed to do some thinking about where he would be setting up his own studio, Simon Duval Architect. Then he remembered that Linda's father owned one of the older Art Deco buildings, Metrocity, in the historic core of the city. Her number was on his mobile phone. Good fortune favoured him as he didn't wait long before she answered.

'Hi, Linda, its me Simon… remember?' he said, teasingly.

'Simon Duval, where have you been, you cad, you promised to phone me weeks ago.'

'Well,' Simon thought quickly, 'that is exactly what I am doing just now.'

'Well?'

'First of all I want to ask you out on a date, but then I also need a favour. I am setting up a new architectural practice and need a good address. Your dad owns the old Metrocity building, and I thought ¼ '

'Hold on there, Simon, before we negotiate a deal for you, what about the first reason for your call? The date you have so glibly passed over?'

He swallowed hard, *Hell this is awkward. I'm tied up for the next few weeks*¼ He had to think fast. Linda was a millionaire's daughter with all the physical attributes, but she was spoilt and liked getting her own way. She was controlling in or out of bed, Simon remembered wryly. He knew his credentials suited her marriage ambitions, but he didn't quite reciprocate the sentiment¼

'Simon? Are you still there?'

'Yes, yes¼ Linda, look the next two weeks look awful, and I am in the throes of getting my show on the road. What can you do for me in the meantime about your dad's building? I promise to get back to you about a date. OK?'

'Simon, you never change, and I don't believe you'll phone me. But I will ask daddy to do something, darling.' She rang off.

He stared out of the window for a few seconds, and pondered the female of the species, The Velvet Club, as he termed it. They could easily be driven to tears, but once having got over the initial disappointment, call it what you will, they would drive a hard bargain, and show a steely toughness to get what they wanted – or get their own back.

Linda did not disappoint and luck was on Simon's side as the premises in the Metrocity building suited his practice perfectly. From the penthouse, with a balcony at each corner, there were views in all directions, showing off the city's breathtaking mountain and bay setting. His new practice, he argued, would get back to basics, architecturally speaking that is, and move away from the glass clad models favoured by developers. The old architects somehow produced designs which were more timeless in their appeal, like this building, whereas the new energy-guzzlers were cheaper to build and usually brought good financial returns only to investors. Simon yearned for the space and time to design from the heart and the mind, freed of expedient solutions. It was now in his power to achieve just that.

His departure from the Atlas Company brought with it some good fortune. First of all his bank account was swelled by the payout of a substantial sum agreed in his contract. Then he had bought sufficient shares in the Company for a directorship had he stayed, that amount now adding up to a tidy sum. He also held shares in the headquarters of the Atlas Company, where an independent assessment of the property showed a considerable increase in real estate terms. With the buy-in of the American real estate developer, his shares had reached even greater value. So, another payout amounting to his share added to his working capital. Financially he was set to go. But with only a few tenuous prospects of work for the future, the new practice was not quite at the starting blocks. On the other hand, now released from the chains of big business, he had time to think. He strutted around his new premises without a care in the world.

Simon's social life was already a complex web in which he could either become ensnared, or remain tactical for the fun of the chase. It couldn't get more complicated. Continually, a voice in his ear reminded him of his unfulfilled promises to his friends of the opposite sex. He had all but forgotten Candice whose voice was now on the other end of the phone line.

'Remember me, Big Boy?' she said huskily.

'Hang on, give me three guesses.'

'OK.'

'Is it Di, no, I mean Wanda, no, I mean Helen¼ '

'No silly, this is Candice.'

'Candice, I knew it all the time, just thought I would get you rattled.'

'It would take a lot more to rattle me, Simon.'

To meet Simon "for old times sake" was her excuse for phoning. That sounded a bit ominous, thought Simon, however he agreed.

Candice was, or rather, should have been from past history. Their brief encounter had only lasted until she went overseas. Her parents were concerned from the start that, from Simon's side, the relationship was not sincere and that he wanted to get closer to the family fortune. Nothing was further from the truth. On the rebound she had got engaged but her fiancè was still overseas.

She greeted him in the same fashion as before, a kiss rather too firm on the lips, which seemed oddly inappropriate. However, it was the same old Candice, outgoing and friendly. As they cruised the coastal road southwards to the Point where the Atlantic and the Indian oceans met, she related her story since they last seen each other. He noticed her engagement ring was absent, and then came her awkward question – had he committed himself to someone else? The possibility of them getting together again was her next question, but before he can respond she played a trump card.

'My father is to invest in a large new project in the city and needs an architect, Simon.'

He recognised a mild form of blackmail and gulped. He saw his life being taken out of his hands and being trapped into renewing the relationship. But, he persuaded himself, he was not inclined to throw away his first commission as Simon Duval Architect.

Simon needed extra hands to free him to design and promote the work of the practice at the topmost level. To get the right design team together, he wasted no time head-hunting for two lean and hungry fledgling architects, Rollo and Tim. Rollo was an architectural technician with advanced computer skills for making fly-through visuals for top class presentations. Tim, on the other hand, was more of a technical boff, able to put the bones of the building together. To complement their skills Simon appointed Stefan, who enjoyed the cut and thrust of the construction site, where he had honed his skills the hard way. With a good team under one roof and with their varied skills they were a perfect combination. It was a good start.

Then he needed a secretary cum executive person to field calls in his absence – and make it seem that his daily schedule is humming with commissions, he mused cynically. Jo worked for him before at the Atlas Company and left for the similar reasons. She could be relied on to hold the fort and with her looks also improve the general ambience of an office. Fortuitously, she applied for the job.

Mr Rosenberg, Candice's father, was a cigar-smoking selfmade man, large of girth which made up for his short height. He seemed to move the world out of his way as he progressed through the office for their first meeting about his new project – Candice's trumpcard.

'Simon, my daughter has sung your praises as an architect, though I think she has a bias in your favour for reasons she only would know about. If this commission goes well, there will be more. I have more open land in the city bowl that cries out for development.' he explained in his clipped English.

The Rosenbergs were Lithuanians by birth who, in their twenties had come to seek a better life in the New World. It was the time of the Depression and they arrived with nothing of real value except their enterprise and spirit to take them to where they longed to be – comfortably off financially. The wine industry of the Cape was their starting point, where they did menial jobs in the cellars of the wine estates, until after ten years they could buy shares in the company where they had employment. Thrift and hard work was their byword. Eventually they owned the major share and could call the shots, finally managing to buy out all other shareholders. Both worked alongside their employees in the assembly line of the cellar, bottling, corking, labelling and packing. They were sitting on a goldmine as the world had awakened to the appeal of the wine of the grape, but it needed savvy to get the product out to the consumer.

The Rosenberg's business drive created a niche market where a case of their wines could be delivered to any doorstep in the country for a nominal sum. Until the market was established they inflicted the same punishing regimen on themselves. They were not given to luxury, and lived modestly, even now. Simon held great admiration for their success.

'Mr Rosenberg, I thank you for the opportunity, your project is assured of my personal attention, and I promise you that you will be satisfied with the final product.'

A large portion of the City was owned by the Rosenbergs, which no other real state developer cared about. High up on the steep slopes of Table Mountain he exposure to high winds, summer and winter, the views were spectacular, and foreign buyers were beginning to stake out the ground for a place in the sun. The Rosenbergs had known all along hat land in the amphitheatre of the city would become scarcer, and in the long term their investment would bear fruit.

Simon's first client, Mr Rosenberg, summarised his brief:

'We want a new apartment building on the slopes of mountain. I don't want expensive building, no, no, no. I want building that is affordable for renting, and therefore affordable to build. Every apartment must face view, and the building must have good looks – you understand what I mean, Mr Duval?'

An architect knows immediately if his client has been around the block a few times, so to speak. Mr Rosenberg had, and he always showed a down-to-earth wisdom, much of which Simon knew he could learn from. He showed Simon photographs of the site and gave a clear brief about the budget. Again Simon was told that this commission could form the first part of a larger commission a little later. Mr Rosenberg was not taking anything for granted and would decide as the work progressed. Perhaps Candice was behind this piecemeal appointment, Simon reasoned –

like the carrot dangling from a stick, until she got what she wanted.

He set about researching the apartment block models coming from Europe at that time, with the team agitating to get their teeth into a new project. So the stage was set for Simon Duval Architects to perform their first act – to change the architectural world and turn it on its head.

"Sense of place" kept cropping up in Simon's head as he tore another fruitless attempt off the sketch pad, rolled it up and sent the missile to the waste bin in the corner of his studio. His attempts had turned up some ideas but nothing really yet that was a good fit for the site. Mr Rosenerg's apartment building, to be known as Southcape needed to satisfy some extreme climatic conditions. The occupants must be able to enjoy shelter from the windy conditions as they went about their daily lives, otherwise the situation could become intolerable for them. As a real estate investment the new complex could suffer a poor reputation before it was completed.

Suddenly the whole picture became clear to him – northern hemisphere models would never satisfy the needs of this site, on the other hand Asian and indigenous African examples might well do so. Rollo was dispatched to the city library to bring back the latest journals, where Simon hoped to find inspiration. *Please let me have some fresh ideas*, he pleaded, closing his hands to the heavens. The noise of the city below at mid-day was intrusive, adding to his sense of futility. He grabbed his coat and told Jo in passing that he needed to clear his head.

Behind the wheel of the Lancia he headed up the last stretch of the tight city network before the open highway. The engine responding pleasingly as with high-pitched revs it overtook the slower traffic clogging the lanes. Following the contour of the Atlantic coastline, the road navigated sharply around the small bay inlets with their white sandy beaches. With few other cars on the road, he gave the car all its power and let down the open top to allow the breeze to play through his hair. He hummed to himself, already feeling the therapy from his escape into the fresh air.

Needing isolation in a familiar place, he headed for a favourite spot, a place where he had taken some of his amours for picnics. He parked, threw off his shoes and socks, then strode across the beach towards nature's own sculpture – a loose jumble of giant granite boulders. Apart from the oyster-catchers scurrying along the waters edge or taking flight as he passed, there was no other life on the beach. He threw down the car rug and lay down to view the world from a fresh angle. With the call of the seagulls as the only other noise above the crash of the breakers on the shoreline, this was the ideal place to refresh and contemplate. *Perfect, for a dose of restorative therapy*, he mused stretching out full length on the rug.

Some hours later Simon had ranged the options for Mr Rosenberg's Southcape project and come to a decision: there were to be no high-rise buildings for Mr Rosenberg, but low-rise, like the courtyard house, dense, compact and private. Above all, the buildings would themselves provide shelter from the wind, and the roof spaces would enjoy the view that Mr Rosenberg so explicitly demanded. Residents' cars could park their cars in communal garages and foot lanes would lead from a central square, like in an Italian village, where the people could interact socially.

Crowded with ideas, Simon swept up the rug and raced across the beach back to the Lancia. He placed a CD of

Vivaldi's Four Seasons in the player and turned up the volume as he headed back to the office. The mood of the music suited his own at that moment.

He burst into the studio and found Rollo, who had returned from the library with the latest in architectural journals and was busy thumbing through them.

'Rollo, I have had an inspiration. The design does not go higher than two storeys, stepped down the slope and catching the view from each level¼ ' He realised that there was someone else in the room.

Rollo nodded his head in the direction of a visitor. There was Diane, looking gorgeous as usual, but completely overdressed for the mid-afternoon. Her jet black hair touched her shoulders and her smooth peach-like complexion enhanced her good looks. She stood tall in her high heels, her turquoise dress fitting her shape to perfection. Untypically, for the moment Simon was lost for words.

Recovering his composure he said, 'Di, great to see you – wow, you look to perfection. How did you find me?'

She paused for a moment so that the full effect of her appearance could be appreciated.

'It isn't hard to find you, Simon. Everyone you know has been trailing you for one thing or another. But guess why I am here.'

'I have no idea, but have some tea – we've got some carrot cake,' Simon offered awkwardly, quietly cursing this interruption in his moment of inspiration. At this stage the others disappeared discreetly from the scene.

'No thanks, Simon, I have come for you to make good on your promise, remember?'

'Yes I do, but this is not a good time for me to leave the office, Di. I have to complete sketches for Mr Rosenberg by twelve noon tomorrow. Let's make it another time, when all this is over.'

'You mean Candice's dad?'

'Yes.'

'You promised me Simon, that you'd stopped seeing Candice. How can I ever believe you again?'

Simon felt cornered again, but typically he found a plausible solution to the immediate bind he was in.

'Tell you what, Di, I'll pick you up at seven tomorrow and we'll do something.'

'Done. Now don't let me down. Promise?' She came to him and planted a kiss on his cheek before swooping out of the door.

One thing he shouldn't lose sight of was that Diane's family owned a wine estate and there could be some commissions from that quarter. *Best to keep in the daughter's good books,* he thought mischievously to himself. His attention returned to the journals and he called the team together.

'Look guys, I had a defining moment this afternoon.' They all raised an eyebrow as they thought of Diane's visit.

Simon picked up the nuance. 'No, you troublemakers, I am talking about the project,' he said shaking his head in mock disbelief.

'In my mind I see not high-rise but low-rise, and the courtyard house. Believe it or not, all these latest journals cover similar concepts successfully completed, mainly in Africa and Asia. There is a move away from high-rise habitation as it turns people into zombies and they get cut off from social life on the ground, more so if it is a long way down to ground level. Don't you see, people need to have their feet on Mother Earth. Then, coming back to the courtyard concept, it creates privacy and real shelter from the elements, ideal for the site we are working on. Sense of place ¼ sense of place, remember?"

Mr Rosenberg liked the ideas very much. He was particularly pleased with the name 'Southcape' that he himself had chosen for the project. For him it evoked a remote and sunny peninsula, surrounded by sea, which in fact described what it was. He talked a lot about the financial side, which was where he was most at home. Simon's sketches paved the way to the second round when Rollo would have a fly-through presentation ready.

After his client's departure, Simon was on a high, and bought cakes for the office in celebration of their first real achievement as a practice. They were all prepared to put in the extra time to beat the deadline, even though Mr Rosenberg had said the programme was flexible. But Simon knew that they must seize the moment and keep the creative juices flowing.

As the sun in the late afternoon began to cast long shadows and leave the city bowl, they decided to work into the night and ordered pizzas from Mr Delivery.

6

Simon's working day started every day with team discussions, followed by definite targets for each particular day. It had been a slow start but there was good progress and Mr Rosenberg was satisfied. That was, until the day he rushed in panting from exertion through the office door.

He greeted Jo in passing but, untypically, walked straight into Simon's office without the usual formalities. Finding Simon there he could hardly contain his distress:

'Simon, there is a problem. A developer bought the ground in front of ours and wants to put up a high-rise apartment block.' Mr Rosenberg's agitation knew no bounds and this new threat to his project caused him to sweat profusely.

'Take a seat Mr Rosenberg. Can I get you something cool to drink?' Mr Rosenberg nodded and Jo hurried off to the tea kitchen.

'Where does this news come from?' Simon enquired quietly, trying to calm his client by remaining calm himself.

'I got the letter from the council saying that zoning - how do you say it? - permits high rise ¼ a tower block if he wishes on that site. All it needs is for¼ consent from the neighbours…we are only one of them,' wheezed a visibly shaken Mr Rosenberg.

'We have council permission for our courtyard concept, Mr Rosenberg., the building plans are all approved, and the contractor has moved on site. There is no way they can permit a scheme that compromises ours. We have priority.'

'Well, they say they can do what suits them – they say the law allows it,' insisted Mr Rosenberg.

'We will object and if necessary we will appeal, sir, on the grounds that our scheme already has approval and their concept would block our views and be an invasion of privacy. All the courts would be visible from a high-rise neighbour. The law disallows obstruction of views, and there are court precedents to prove it.'

'Precisely,' offered the client, but not entirely convinced. 'Now then, Simon, you must do something! I give full permission for you to write a letter on my behalf.'

Who are these people?, questioned Simon to himself.

A worried Mr Rosenberg took his leave and Simon got to the Lancia and drove hellbent to beat the council's closing time. *Heaven knows those with sheltered employment tend to cut corners on the hours of the working days*, he muttered under his breath. He arrived in time, but only to confirm that Mr Rosenberg's information was correct: the applicant was the new Atlas Company with its American partner which intended pursuing their high-rise building plans on the site in front of Southcape. With two consenting signatures already in the bag, the way could be clear for their high-rise building. *Oh no*, thought Simon accepting the challenge, *you haven't matched wits with the real Duval yet!* On the other hand he figured, a fight with his old company could prove entertaining…

'I tendered for the Southcape project, and was lucky enough to be accepted,' Nick told Dr Stephens during his second session. Mr Rosenberg seemed especially pleased to have a builder who Simon knew. We moved on site with our builders' huts and stores and erected them neatly in the one corner and secured the site with fencing all round. At night temporary floodlighting lit the builder's yard and a night watch stationed in one of the huts. Like Simon, I was equally disturbed that the council could be swayed by invisible pressures, as had quite often happened in the past, and the Atlas high-rise could go head.

'We took stock daily as to progress, Simon at the council, and me checking for any sign of action on the Atlas site. A month after the distressing discovery, Simon was summoned to the council offices to meet the chief of city planning, a Mr Jennings. He personally was managing the progress of the Atlas Company's plans application. It was a concerned Mr Jennings greeted him civilly then declared that a third adjoining owner had agreed to the Atlas Company's plans, and that Mr Rosenberg's signature was the last one needed. Knowing the lengths to which the Atlas Company would go to secure anything they wanted, backhanders were not unlikely, Simon reasoned. Mr Jennings was told that, under no circumstances would Mr Rosenberg agree to the depreciation of his project just to please the Atlas Company, and a lawyer's letter would be on its way. The situation had reached an ominous juncture.

'On a morning when all things seemed to be going right, I phoned to report to Simon that security fencing had been erected overnight on the Atlas site. The nightwatch reported that a large team of subcontractors had worked under cover of darkness. Knowing the law, Simon arranged for a court order to prevent the Atlas Company from building until all the approvals are in place. Not long, and a call came from the Atlas chief, proving Simon's intuition to be right…'

'Simon, my dear fellow, where have you been all this time? You know we have never been able to replace your particular blend of skills in the Company. Is there a chance you might consider an offer?'

'Thanks a lot, but no thanks,' retorted Simon, remaining distant and offhand.

'Well, now, I see you are doing so well, it is not surprising that you prefer to work for yourself. Yes?'

'Quite so.'

'We have a little problem, which I am sure you will know about. Your client, Mr Rosenberg, is always out of communication. We can never reach him and the directors felt that I should rather approach you about the approval of our plans. You know Simon, we have influence at Council and this could also work in your favour if you could lean on Mr Rosenberg for us. Our American partner has bought up other sites in the city, and has the backing from top level. You see, their local man is the American ambassador, Mr Quaid. With those credentials only good can come for the city. We need Mr Rosenberg's consent use to proceed. Naturally we would make it worth your while¼ '

Simon fumed at the insinuation that he would consider a bribe.

'No, sir, there is no way that I will bring pressure to bear on my client, which is what you are asking, in order to save your project. I don't have divided loyalties in this matter, and you can keep your bribe for the costs of any law suit which might arise from furthering your company's self-interest at the expense of my client's interests.'

'I am sorry you feel that way, Simon. Then we shall have no alternative but to resort to Plan B, which is more radical I'm afraid.'

'That sounds like a veiled threat, if I might say so. And, by the way, whose backing do you have at top level?' There was silence at the other end. Simon put the phone down. He felt distinctly uneasy about the way things were going.

Chapter Three

On another day and in another part of the city, the Anglican Archbishop of the Cape, the Very Reverend. Anthony Hitchcock, was holding sway over the meeting of the Synod. His frustration knew no bounds as the parish had grown to a point where it needed a building of stature. On important days on the church calendar the worshipping flock, which came from far and wide, had to squeeze into the old stone church. It had become completely inadequate and a building for a congregation of twice the size would be more suitable. Better still, building a new house of worship closer to the congregants was his preference.

At this meeting – one of many – he was determined to get the trucculent footdraggers in the Synod to finally agree to funding a new cathedral in a good location, but also to elevate the status of the Church of the Province in the public eye. There was no point in delaying it any longer, his eminence argued for the umpteenth time, and he was confident that the funding would come with the assistance of Canterbury in England.

Using a bit of guile to circumvent the perennial delaying tactics of some members who had served on the Synod for decades, the 'Arch', the name by which he was affectionately known, finally achieved his goal, and his project got the nod.

With a sense of triumph he picked up the telephone and dialled the number of the architectural profession's institute. He introduced himself to the secretary. He wanted, he said importantly, the best person in the profession to prepare the documents for an open competition for architects, and who could advise on a suitable jury. The experience of a senior architect, Mr Brian Dawson, in such matters couldn't be bettered, he was told. The Arch delayed no longer in soliciting the help of Mr Dawson, who happened to be an Anglican, in setting up a competition for a new Cathedral. The competition was to be announced through the Press, together with an invitation to all architects who wished to participate. A date for the collection of competition documents and payment of deposits would be made known.

Not given to much social interaction within the profession (due to the undoubted sense of rivalry within the fraternity which spoils such occasions), the participating architects were thrown together at an inaugural function where the documents were handed out. Simon Duval was amongst them. There is a new face around town and Simon observed that she had an aura of strutting confidence and was expensively dressed in the best labels. He, and some other members of the profession were keen to make the acquaintance of Ms Catherine Quaid, but, while all were still in their seats, she left the room.

Simon returned to the studio and called the team together.

'I know we are all doing overtime on the Southcape project, but, that will be coming to an end one day not too far off, and we need another good project. I believe that the Anglican Cathedral competition, even if we don't win, will bring a fresh breeze into our work routine, and stimulate our creative juices. What about it everyone?'

About participating in the Cathedral competition, there was no hesitation, which was what Simon really liked about his team. They were hungry for creative opportunities and accepted any challenge willingly. They shared the design philosophy that 'the whole is a sum of the parts', which simply meant that, as with music, good design demanded that the main theme of the design should be echoed in all the parts – even the smallest of detail in a building was worthy of their attention. Many acclaimed historical examples portrayed this approach, which strengthened their own design convictions. The converse would be a mishmash of ideas which did not add up to an architecture of worth, and regrettably an approach which characterised much of the work coming out of some of the esteemed design studios of the world.

'However,' Simon reminded them unnecessarily, 'Southcape still presents us with day to day problems, no less the unaccounted for failure of part of its structure.'

He had hardly finished the sentence when Nick called him to the site. The nightwatch had seen some movement during the night – a turn of events which would shed more light on the structural collapse at Southcape.

The nightwatch said he went to investigate a noise and startled an intruder with explosives, this time at another corner of the building. The intruder escaped and he immediately called "boss Nick", who took possession of the explosives.

Simon raced to the site and found Nick surveying the damage.

'Look here, Simon, these fresh tracks lead to the fence,' Nick said pointing to the ground as he paced off towards the fence. 'Hold on, here is something peculiar,' he added, and 'the ground here has been disturbed. And what's this?'

Lifting the edge of a caste iron cover, Nick revealed a hole. On lifting it higher a brick-lined tunnel running down the slope could be seen in the murky darkness.

'Of course,' he said snapping his fingers, 'this is the disused water conduit under the city. It's historic and constructed probably to provide water in the early days, and maybe even to the castle moat.'

They eased themselves down to the floor of the circular tunnel, just high enough in which to stand upright.

The connection with the explosives began to dawn on them. The tunnel declined in the direction of the Atlas Company's site. Staring into the darkness they could see a ladder, where light fell on the metal rungs. The plot began to dawn on them: the perpetrator had gained access to their site through the tunnel and was able plant the explosives on the Southcape site.

Nick looked at Simon: 'This looks like war, pal. Your old friends at Atlas are wanting to scupper Southcape's viability by destabilising the structure – the bad publicity would do the rest. I guess this is their spiteful response to not getting Mr Rosenberg's signature.

The logic was obvious and Simon nodded in agreement.

Mr Rosenberg, on hearing Simon's report was, on the one hand, relieved that the initial collapse of the structure was not due to shoddy building, and on the other determined to get the perpetrators to court. The police were called to investigate and shown photos of the first collapse and the blackened evidence, and the explosives for the second attempt. During the routine investigation, the directors of the Atlas Company were questioned about the company's possible involvement. Linking the Atlas Company to the incident was going to prove difficult as they brought in their legal guns to defend any case against them. But, an element of suspicion persisted due to the continued stand-off between Mr Rosenberg and the Atlas Company board over their high-rise project. There was indeed a motive. All that was needed was to connect the Atlas Company to the incident.

Assistance came from an unexpected quarter.

At the time of slavery in the Cape, some slaves deserted their owners at great risk to their lives taking refuge in the mountain forests around the new settlement. In modern times, descendents of these slaves were commonly called the true Cape "bluebloods" due to their claim to a long lineage under the shadow of Table Mountain – yet they are vagrants, most of whom spent much of their lives in a twilight zone of inebriaton. They roved the city under cover of darkness, unwittingly providing the police with a helpful network of informants. Generally, their own reputation for committing crime was unfounded, and incongruous though it may seem, they lived by a code of reporting crime whenever they saw it. Except in extreme cases did they themselves break the law, more to survive than out of greed. Otherwise they were the flotsam of humanity and generally harmless.

Before the week was at an end, a vagrant Silas, was brought in by his peers for police questioning.

'Silas,' asked his interrogator, 'can't you stay out of trouble?'

'Nay, meneer, its the devil always makes me do it.' Silas pulled himself up in his chair as if he had disposed of an awkward question, or so he thought.

'Why have your friends brought you to the police station, Silas. Is it about the explosives?'

'Ja, meneer.'

Silas admitted to accepting payment for placing the explosives during both incidents at Southcape.

'Who paid you to do this, Silas. And where did you get the explosives?'

'Meneer, this boss came in a big car to where I sleep in the street. It was a big black car, like an American car…'

'And it had a flag…' added his companion.

'His driver gave me some money, then told me where to pick up the charge. I mustn't tell anyone he told me. He tell me how to get into the tunnel down the ladder from the one side, and move the ladder to get up the other side. Then I must put down the charges, and go back before putting a match to the fuse. But, before I could do all this stuff, the nightwatchman saw me, and I run away in a hurry and left the charge there. Am I in trouble, meneer?'

Silas was let off with a warning. His evidence provided the criminal court with conclusive evidence against the Atlas Company which was successfully prosecuted and the company paid the price for perpetrating deliberate damage to property. The sentence was a year in goal for the chairman of the company, alternatively a fine of one hundred thousand rand. The fine was paid without hesitation and the controversial high-rise development was given the thumbs down by the same court, without leave to appeal. Silas's disclosure about American involvement raised questions about the ambassador's role in the attempted sabotage of the Southcape development.

On meeting Simon outside the courtroom, Candice linked arms with him and pecked him on the cheek. 'Congratulations, clever boy,' she teased.

It was late afternoon, and Nick and Estrella would be meeting them at the Cove to enjoy sundowners together, then they would go on to celebrate with dinner together at a restaurant somewhere along the Atlantic seaboard. The backdrop of the crashing breakers between the granite islands and the seagulls hovering on the late afternoon sea breeze set a mellow mood for relaxation after the intensity of the trial. Nick popped the champagne and the inevitable post-mortem of the trial followed. It was like dealing with grief, a way of purging themselves once and for all of the bizarre circumstances and motives behind the episode now finally behind them.

The initial negative publicity for Southcape had been turned on its head, but Simon still harboured one last niggling worry: The Atlas Company's plans with American backing were turned down by the council by order of the court, but there would be retribution of some kind somewhere down the track. Ambassador Quaid was an elusive figure but was he the power behind the throne. He wondered where and how revenge would surface.

Nick and Estrella left Simon and Candice at the Cove to watch the last light of day. Candice was close and loving and Simon felt completely at the mercy of the moment. They were reluctant to leave this magical spot, spoke little and lingered to well after dark. Eventually through implication Candice suggested a change of mood: 'Your place or mine?' she said.

Simon awoke alone to the start of a new day. His bachelor pad resembled a tip, and his mirror advised him that his over-indulgence of the night before was not doing his good looks any favours. It would be a good idea to get to the gym sometime, he mused, while doing a raincheck on his well-sculpted physique. He showered slowly and then dresses casually. Today he was scheduled to meet at the city church to make notes for the Cathedral competition. His meeting was with Reverend Ambrose who would go through the competition brief with him so that he can make more informed design decisions. At this stage he didn't have any preconceived ideas, preferring to keep his mind open and clear so that he could start with a clean slate.

The site chosen for the diocese's future flagship was on the periphery of the city in a place known as the Cape Flats. The old house of worship in the centre city with its beautifully crafted stone vaulting had served the city for a century but with the growth of the new outlying suburbs it had become too difficult for the majority of congregants to reach. It would remain and continue to function in tandem with its new sibling on the Flats.

The trademark aesthetic of the Anglican churches with its timeless message of permanence over the generations was what Simon wanted to capture in his design. In times quite different from those of old, it was essential, he felt, for the church-goers to have a house of worship which could compete successfully for attendance when there were so many other attractions - or distractions. Much to the concern of the church hierarchy, attendance numbers were down. Like landmark buildings, such as the Sydney Opera House and the Guggenheim Museum in Bilboa, a fine piece of contemporary architecture for the Cathedral could become a drawcard for more worshippers and visitors to the city.

During his travels Simon had enjoyed firsthand experience of some of the finest church architecture in Europe: Gaudi's Sagrada Familia in Barcelona, Auguste Peret's Church of Notre Dame de Raincy in Paris, Le

Corbusier's Ronchamp chapel in France and Basil Spence's Coventry Cathedral in England. Older Spanish cathedrals like at Santiago and Avila in Spain drew people in a kind of pilgrimage to them. The question was why? Broadly the answer must be their intrinsic beauty which people sensed on entry - people were drawn to quality, not just cosmetic but genuine. The church building was a space conducive to worship and it needed to be awe-inspiring, to uplift the downtrodden, be soothing to the troubled, and relieve the worriers of their suffering. All these experiential responses were a huge challenge to any architect, and Simon drew his breath when thinking about the enormity of the task.

A good time to steer the mind into conceptual thought was in the waking hours, before the world bombarded the senses with mundane demands. It seemed ironic to Simon that he enjoyed such clarity of mind in between sleep and being awake. That morning he lay peacefully exploring the ideas which flooded his head. For the first time he would be creating architectural space with spiritual qualities - where functionality was subservient to abstractness. He toyed with symbolism, turning over geometric and free-form shapes in his mind and explored alternative ideas in his search for the right spatial form.

He snapped his fingers suddenly, as if to cement the idea firmly before it eluded him: *Of course, the egg!* First of all, he reasoned, the egg was a geometric form, but at the same time it was an organic shape. *Perfect*, its metaphor was obvious. The egg represented the beginning of a life form, needing only to be fertilised. The congregation, the worshippers, could bring that life to the Cathedral. It all seemed so completely pre-ordained that the body of the church should emerge from an eggshaped footprint, with high walls kept sheer to enhance the clarity of the symbolism.

Natural light, and how to coax it into the interior of this profound embryonic vision, preoccupied his mind. He swayed around under the shower, considering how, for the short time spent under a shower, there was a brief but complete isolation from the world around. It was almost like a baptism transporting one to a higher level and restoring the jaded earthly being to a renewed freshness. Was this a quality needed for the house of worship? Simon began to think so.

Architects were fond of bringing their ideas into three dimensional form with scale models. At Simon Duval Architect, models of the Cathedral concept in cardboard made by Rollo and Tim mounted up at one end of the studio. Each one a stage in the evolution of a single idea - the egg form. The theme was developing, with skylights pouring light through a structural tracery and washing the solid heavily textured nave walls from above. At the lower level, where the congregation sat, the natural light would have diminished and deep geometric openings with thick brightly coloured glass would penetrate the solid walls. The glow of colour at the human level would evoke a sense of well-being.

All this was about the body of the Cathedral itself, but Simon was already a step ahead, exploring ideas to dramatise the building's stately presence.

When he arrived at the studio, the latest model of the egg-shaped plan form and vertical walls was being scrutinised critically by team. They gathered for the morning session as Simon cleared the table and picking up a flat box, placed it in the centre of the expansive surface. He took the new model placing it on top to illustrate the point he is about to make.

'By giving the Cathedral an elevation above the world around, it would be much like the cathedral complexes in medieval cities.' he explained.

He went on: 'This is the elevation above the street that I want for the main body. The Cathedral's floor should not be at ground level, but stand on a podium, some storeys high. Around the main body the vestry and the projecting side chapels together with the external buttresses for the high walls would soften the external profile. The half-basement level would become known as the Crypt, a social space for the church to provide shelter for street people and others who are needy.

'Then, access to the Cathedral would be up a long and wide flight of steps, interrupted only with wide landings, all of which could serve for outdoor assemblies. Other easier means of access could be by a winding ramp and elevators. The seminary and the diocesan office, and the Arch's rooms could then find a place somewhere in the podium.'

There was genuine appreciation from the team for Simon's inspiration. The design was enhanced considerably by the podium and could be a winner. Rollo and Tim could hardly wait for the morning session to end and to start modelling the final version for the competition.

Catherine Quaid set up a round of interviews of prospective staff for her architectural practice. She had a very clear idea about the sort of skills she was looking for and contacted the architectural faculty to find out who were the best final year students of that year. She also knew someone at the profession's institute with information about qualified architects looking for work.

Her first appointment was Mandy as her executive secretary (the title Catherine preferred for the position). In executive terms, Mandy, like Catherine, was known as a 'power dresser' – she wore two piece suits to work, stockings and low-heeled shoes. She, like Catherine, wore her hair short and well-cut by the best salon in the city. Together they interviewed the candidates, and in time Catherine began to rely more and more on Mandy's judgement about their potential as staff members in her practice. Characteristically they felt more comfortable with the female applicants, two of whom, Debbie and Sandy were appointed to start immediately. The third architect was Ralph (whom Catherine preferred to call 'Rafe').

Catherine had grown up in New York. Her father's postings as ambassador to countries in the Third World amply qualified him for his new position in the Cape Town embassy. The family was connected with a prominent banking group in the United States and exceedingly wealthy. Catherine was an only child and had grown into a well-groomed good-looking woman with a strikingly pale complexion and green eyes under dark eyebrows. Her short auburn hair framed her narrow features. She was the apple of her father's eye and been a success at everything she had undertaken since childhood. Her training with the 'greats' in architecture, such as Paul Rudolph, at the Yale art and architecture faculty. Not lacking in self-confidence. she set up her architectural practice in the Cape and started to play the cocktail circuit. Her love of fine art was shared with her mother, and she knew as much about the great masters as she did about architecture, a valuable conversation topic in the circles in which the Quaids moved.

Ambassador Quaid ensured that his daughter had the best location for her practice, and funded her lease of the penthouse suite on the top floor of the tallest building in the city, Imperial Heights. The spacious interior was soon transformed into an impressive reception area with a marble floor, glass enclosed meeting rooms with soft carpets and furnishings and a drawing office, completely coccooned without natural light to create a controlled environment for the computer operatives.

The new practice was launched with a party for invited guests amongst whom wre all the ambassadors resident in the city, parliamentarians, officials from the city council and a handful of favoured family friends.

Catherine was radiant and the archetypal American hostess, making small talk to keep the conversation flowing easily. The works of some of her architectural mentors graced the walls and were always useful conversation pieces. Some of her father's favourite paintings by Miro, Matisse and Cezanne were displayed in prominent places and naturally drew the attention of the moneyed gathering.

Not lost on a sense of occasion, and at the precisely correct moment, Catherine tapped three times on a wine glass and commenced to welcome her guests.

'Wonderful friends, it gives me enormous pleasure to see you here at the launch of my new practice. I thank you all for coming. But I have also to thank daddy whose generosity knows no bounds. He has been my most solid support in transforming these premises into a place which will soon be buzzing with architectural commissions.

'Then my mother who is a stalwart and I think I owe any artistic sensitivity I might have to her. She did the floral arrangements with flowers from the embassy gardens. Don't forget, any commission is not too small, but of course the big ones pay the rent! Please enjoy yourselves this evening and don't hurry away.'

In a very short time Catherine's practice had numerous commissions for upmarket residences for her parent's well-to-do friends, located mainly in the 'stockbroker belt', in the upper reaches of a leafy suburb. The buildings she designed for them were stylish versions of the architecture with which she is familiar from back home in the States. However, the Cathedral competition was a high profile project and therefore a great opportunity to launch herself as an architect in the upper echelons of the profession which could in time bring international recognition. In America she had been brought up in the episcopalian tradition which was akin to the Anglican denomination in terms of its doctrine as well as some liturgical overlaps. She felt well up to the challenge and she made the Cathedral competition her priority. The hand-in date was only a few weeks away.

A good supply of research material from America was ordered before she would allow herself to contemplate design ideas for the competition. Her experience of the American counterparts included some of the spectacular steel and glass houses of worship in California, where buildings take on the appearance of multiple glass prisms using clever technology that defy gravity – awe-inspiring from both the outside and the inside. The idea of a cut diamond invaded her thoughts repeatedly and it was with considerable difficulty that she was able to concentrate on the other work in the office.

Her style as the boss was that all morning sessions were to be recorded in minutes, so that each member of the team had a clear brief for each working day. Mandy presided over the meetings freeing Catherine to be the designer supremo. The young architects were intrigued with the verbal descriptions of her concept, but had to wait for Catherine's ideas to appear on paper. There was clearly going to be a delay as her first sketches were conspicuous by their absence.

After days of unproductive searching for ideas, Catherine felt she needed to know how other candidates are faring before she herself could commit herself. Another thought consoled her in her frustration: the ambassador knew one or two members of the jury, which in itself would not be a disadvantage, she reasoned, especially if she ran short of time and a possible extension of time could be arranged.

A notice appearing in the architects' journal with a telephone number caught her eye: *Modelmaker needed for fast track project. Contact Simon Duval Architect.* Catherine recalled meeting Simon briefly at the inauguration of the competition. She thought him to be rather handsome, with a sort of aura about him which spelt confidence and success and, if one was to stereotype an architect, he epitomised her idea of one.

Catherine lifted eyes from the page, stood up and began to pace the room. She had reached a mental block with the Cathedral project and needed to know what the other competitors were doing, so that she knew what she was up against to get her creative juices flowing. The prospect of winning always excited her. Until then she had felt mired down without any particular way forward. *But*, she schemed silently to herself, *if I lend Rafe, the model maker, to Duval we would have the inside track on at least one design - that would at least provide a sort of catalyst to break the logjam.*

Ralph was duly summoned to the boardroom, and advised to take temporary paid leave and persuaded to apply for the advertised temporary position at Duval's office. Catherine made some excuse about a lull in the office programme, but, he was assured, his position would be kept open for him once the competition was over. However, under no circumstances was he allowed to disclose his employment with Catherine Quaid. Thus decided, thus done, and Ralph, without any suspicion of a motive, was appointed by Simon to help specifically with the construction of the Cathedral model in his studio.

A week passed without word from Ralph. Mandy recalled him to the office on some pretext so that Catherine could prompt responses from him about the Duval design, of which by now he should have an intimate knowledge. Her suspicions were confirmed – the way Ralph described the Duval design it did indeed have merit and was probably going to end up in the top layer of the submissions. The upside was that she felt distinctly better equipped to proceed with a concept, maybe similar to that described by Ralph, but not obviously so. *That is for the jury to sort out*, she reasoned.

'Thankyou, Rafe, for coming in and good luck with the model. We miss not having you here with us, but all for a good cause, I can assure you,' she told him distractedly. Ralph, a straightforward uncomplicated youth, suspected nothing about being a pawn in Catherine's dubious scheming.

With a new focus, Catherine arrived early at the office the next day. She had abandoned her suit in favour of a smock, and tied her hair back in two tufts, transforming, even softening her appearance. Her green eyes shone with anticipation as she shared her upbeat mood with Mandy.

'Today I am going to spend the entire day sketching out ideas for the Cathedral and I don't want to take any calls, unless it is a new client of course.'

The staff was duly instructed not to disturb her and the office settled into a routine of making no demands on her time. She liked to think that her inspiration would be the Californian examples, hybridised to suit the local cultural landscape, but as there was so much good sense in what Duval was doing, it was hard to remove her creative mind away from the images which Ralph had described, even in his inarticulate way.

Towards mid-afternoon Catherine faced mounds of discarded paper around her in the studio. With her sketches in soft pencil she was making headway, she felt, and was excited about the egg-shape which she had remodelled 'deconstructively'.

The pure form of the egg was obliterated with jagged openings slashed at angles down the vertical walls. These would be filled with glass she envisaged. Her conclusion was that the Duval concept made a great deal of sense, but to her it lacked theatrical effect, but it was increasingly difficult not to copy too closely some of the other features, such as elevating the entire body of the Cathedral, and surrounding it with the ancillary functions.

At the end of the day, her conceptual sketches were revealed to the staff with a flourish and Ralph was summoned for a further debriefing.

His Worship, the 'Arch' arrived with an entourage to view the hanging of the entries and to join the jury in the diocesan boardroom afterwards. All the scale models were laid out on the boardroom table, presenting a fascinating agglomeration of ideas – two of them, they noticed, are strikingly similar and there is some speculation as to whether they were from the same architect - or just variations on a theme. However, the competition rules precluded more than one entry per participant, and that was that.

After a week of deliberation, and overwhelmed with the quality of the submissions, the jury exhausted its discussions and proceeded to filter out the 'also-rans' for a shortlist of five finalists. Both practices, those of Duval and Quaid had made it through to the last five, then to the last three, and finally the Arch opened the sealed envelope of the jury's final choice and announced:

'The winner is Mr Simon Duval Architect. I must thank the jury most sincerely for chosing the design which happens to be the one I believe encapsulates precisely what I had in mind for the new cathedral of St Francis of Assisi. Shall we call the architect to the boardroom for an official announcement?'

Simon kept pacing the floor of the studio. He had a sneaking suspicion that the phone call from the diocesan secretary requesting him to come to the diocesan office was auspicious, but he contained his optimism until the cat is in the bag. He arrived at the diocesan office in double quick time. The Arch, enjoying the privilege of breaking the news, met him at the door as he entered:

'Mr Duval, may I congratulate you on your winning entry. I am delighted with what you have designed for us. You have empathised in concrete with the needs of the church so magnificently that I believe we have a new icon in church architecture. Well, done. Do come and meet the jury.'

In keeping with the Arch's habit of herding along his flock, he steered Simon gently to the jury table, where he was greeted with handshakes and introduced to each member. His first impression was the predominance of elder churchmen, although there are a few younger appointees to the panel headed by the architect who compiled the competition, Mr Brian Dawson.

At the jury's request, Simon explained the nuances of his design. They sat in rapt attention, but plied him with questions about how the various functions would fit in as well as about financing of the project. The jury particularly favoured the idea of the Crypt becoming a social venue for the needy.

'All very appropriate, given the role of the church in uplifting those who have fallen by the wayside,' said the Arch swelling with magnanimity. He went on: 'Now, Mr Duval, can you explain why there is another scheme which virtually replicates your design, although I personally don't believe that it has the clarity and purity of yours? However, members of the jury believe it has merit and have awarded it second place.'

Simon was shown the other design which uncannily echoed his concept of the egg-form even down to details in some areas. It was uncannily similar in form but differed in so far as it looked as though someone had taken an axe and altered the purity of shape – *ah, these deconstructivists*, he thought to himself, *they take a simple concept and fragment it purely for effect*. He was at loss to explain to the jury the similarity of the basic concept. He did notice however, a breach of the competition rules - no identity markings. What he saw was a tiny logo of two crossed-over gloved hands in the bottom right hand corner.

He shrugged, and shook his head, 'I am sorry, I have no idea. It is astonishingly similar, I agree, but has to be coincidence.' But to Simon there had to be a more rational explanation than pure coincidence. He enquired about the author of the second entry. 'Ms Catherine Quaid,' informed one of the jurors, 'but that is just between us for the time being.'

The outcome of the Cathedral competition reached Catherine in a hand-delivered letter from the diocesan office, informing her that her design had been placed second. She greeted the news with initial stoicism, which concealed her inner fury at having not managed to outsmart the other participants. Failure to win is not in her book, never had been, never will be. *Duval's design was bland, boring, lacking tension, untrendy, and, let's use the word, unsexy!* She figured that her application of deconstructivist principles to the organic egg form achieved all those things and more. How could a jury be so blind to those shortcomings in their chosen scheme?

Her father despaired when he heard the news. Ambassador Quaid decided that through their social connections he should at least try to get a review of the choice. The two schemes were so close at the finish that the individual jurists might have been swayed into a consensus, he argued to himself, whereas each one might have decided quite differently had it come to the vote. Furthermore, since the Archbishop had been to cocktails at the embassy on numerous occasions, he felt he has a good entrè there. He would start at the top, as is the custom of the Quaids when they really wanted something.

He consoled Catherine:

'My dear, the outcome hasn't yet been made public, but there is no time to lose. I will call on the Archbishop and suggest an independent review, after all this is so important to the whole image of the church. Maybe we could suggest that the Episcopalian church in the States might be persuaded to finance the costs of the interior embellishment, which will undoubtedly be very high. This would only happen if your design is chosen, of course.'

Catherine hugged her father for being so supportive and returned to her studio. She waltzed into the reception, and called Mandy to buy cakes all round.

'Please, only chocolate,' she insisted, 'chocolate always drives out negative thoughts. Think of it Mandy, just the possibility that the outcome of the competition will be overturned after an independent review, fills me with hope, and I feel a lot better. My entry was second, which means if the result is overturned – which one is next in line? Mine of course.'

From his spacious office overlooking the bay, Catherine's father fumed over the phone at the diocesan secretary whom he believed was obstructing his calls to the Archbishop.

'I apologise, ambassador Quaid, but there is nothing more that I can do about it. The Archbishop is heavily engaged in discussions with an international donor for a chain of soup kitchens for the needy people on the Cape Flats, and those negotiations have reached a delicate stage.'

'Very well, then,' the ambassador deciding to cool down, 'but see to it that you get him on the phone the moment he is free. Good day.'

Ambassador Quaid's persistence raised the Arch's antler-like eyebrows. *What the deuce could be so urgent?* In his own time he placed a call and got the ambassador on the line.

'Good morning, Archbishop, how kind of you to return my calls.'

'Good morning Ambassador. There seems to be something urgent which you would like to discuss?'

'Well, good sir, it is urgent only in as much as the announcement¼ '

'Announcement?'

'Yes, Archbishop, the announcement of the jury's current choice from the Cathedral entries. I am concerned that unless there is an independent review of the jury's decision, that the church will never be sure that it made the right choice in the first place.'

'What are you suggesting, Ambassador – that we start the whole jury process all over again?'

'That would be one option, good sir, but I don't want to be prescriptive. Another would be to canvas public opinion before a choice is made.'

Quite certain of his opinion that the worshippers would prefer their Cathedral to be adorned lavishly and sumptuously, the ambassador continued:

'Then, of course, Archbishop, I shall do all I can to persuade the Episcopalian church in the States to become a substantial donor to the project, perhaps pay for the high cost of the interior décor, or maybe even to your soup kitchen project. I understand you are busy with that as a priority¼ at the present time¼ am I right?'

'I will convey your suggestion to the competition organisers, Ambassador, but at this stage let me state quite emphatically, that I am personally very taken with the jury's choice, and it would need a lot of persuasion to change my mind. I will let you know whether they will consider your proposal, and what they decide.'

The Archbishop put down the phone and rolled his eyes to the ceiling. It is as though once again he was having to lean on the jury to ensure his will prevailed. Still fuming, he arranged to meet with the jury as scheduled for that afternoon, to get this new intrusion over with as soon as possible.

Simon was deep in thought when the phone rang on his studio desk. Jo took the call.

'The chairman of the Cathedral jury is on the line, Simon, he wants you to go down to the diocesan office right away, if possible. Can I tell him you are on your way?'

Sitting around the large board room table was the entire jury as well as His Worship, looking peeved, or so it seemed to Simon. The jury comprised professional architects, some who held posts at the universities and amongst them was the persuasive group of senior parishioners, all of whom put the church's interests before their own. They were of the sort who don't give into presssure of any kind, however, the offer of American finance for the soup kitchen programme put another complexion on things. The fact that the American ambassador's daughter, Catherine, was one of the finalist, whose entry did not win their vote only made the situation more delicate and complex, to say the least.

Noting their ambivalence, the Archbishop became more and more concerned that the jury might be swayed by this new carrot labelled 'soup kitchens' dangling before their eyes, and that Simon's winning proposal – his personal choice - would be sacrificed on the altar of expediency.

After much deliberation, they found what they believed to be a possible compromise, but it all hinged on the winner: Simon Duval Architect who would have to agree.

The chairman opened the discussion.

'Mr Duval, thankyou for coming at such short notice. We have had hard and long discussions about your entry and indeed, we are certain that our choice has been the right one. However, as a man of the world, you will of course understand that churches everywhere have to remain viable in all their diverse initiatives while saving souls, and it just so happens that there is an offer of money from the United States - yet to be confirmed – for the funding of the Archbishop's soup kitchen project.

'What has this all to do with me? questioned Simon to himself.

'Well, as you are aware, the American ambassador's daughter, Catherine Quaid, submitted a proposal which, by the way is very similar to your own – yes? - but the jury feels it lacked the modesty of yours.'

'It was uncanny,' said Simon, still mystified.

Then the wheels began to turn in his mind, and in a flash Simon believed he knew the answer – *That's it, Ralph was the interloper, maybe unwittingly, but he knew all about our design. And, to top it all he is now back at Catherine Quaid's office.* For the time being Simon kept this revelation to himself.

'To open the way for the American money, we were wondering,' continued the chairman, 'whether you would be prepared to meet the church's dilemma half-way and consider combining forces with the Ambassador's daughter, Ms Quaid, to work on the project together. After all, your designs are so similar, almost with the same genes¼ ,' he looked around for at least a sign of support from the other members present. None appeared to be forthcoming.

To Simon the idea was anathema – first of all to share the scheme with anyone held no appeal, secondly he disliked the adulterated version of his design Catherine had produced, and finally, she was guilty of industrial or professional espionage, call it what you like, but a crime in his eyes.

'I am afraid not, sir. For the jury's information, I have just thought of a possible – I repeat "possible" - explanation for the similarity of our schemes. Catherine Quaid's employee, a young man called Ralph, answered an advertisement I placed for a temporary modelmaker. I never suspected for one moment that it might lead to what is known in business circles as industrial espionage. This might explain why the two schemes are the so similar.'

He explained further how Ralph, a naïve lad, could have become an unwitting interloper between the two offices.

However speculative this conclusion was, the air in the diocesan boardroom was pregnant with a prolonged silence. But the jury comprised men of the world and the newspapers every day carried reports of humankind's conduct, good or bad. Simon's explanation about a possible interloper to them, although unproven, was indeed plausible. Eventually the chairman, broke the silence, thanked Simon for his time, and shook his hand at the door, 'Thankyou again for coming, Mr Duval. We shall be in contact with you soon.'

After Simon's departure, all around the table turned to the Arch – after all the sins of mankind were his department.

'I think I have heard enough,' he said, raising his large purple clad form from his seat. 'Even a suspicion of plagiarism is sufficient to cast doubt on the Quaid entry. Therefore, I would like to jury to reaffirm its choice of the

Duval design. The suggestion of possible donor money for the soup kitchens is not a firm offer, and I would implore the jury not to be diverted from its task, that is, to choose the design which in fact carries my vote.'

With this assertive stand, the Arch aimed to steer the jury away from any change of mind about the best Cathedral project. Who, in his right mind, would go against the head of the church after all?

The more Simon speculated about the possibility of plagiarism, the more he fumed. He called Ralph saying he needed him for one more afternoon, just to tidy up the model room, and broached the subject of the competition. His suspicions were confirmed when Ralph conceded that Simon's scheme had in fact been discussed with Catherine. In all innocence he, Ralph, had not realised that he was being used as a source of information for Catherine's nefarious purposes.

After Simon's departure from the diocesan boardroom, the Arch left the jury behind closed doors so that the members could decide on their best course of action. They concluded that the evidence was too thin to disqualify Catherine Quaid's entry, and in any event to do so would lead to a hue and cry which the church could well do without. Catherine, too, could challenge their decision in court, and jointly and individually they might be accused of defamation, a prospect that none of them relished.

To the great satisfaction of the Arch, the jury confirmed its original choice of the Cathedral project of Simon Duval Architect, and so from then onwards the project took on a life of its own. But the spectre of Catherine Quaid's duplicity would continue to haunt Simon's professional life.

The roofwetting ceremony for Southcape, Mr Rosenberg's pride and joy, was by invitation only and arranged for the late afternoon, after working hours.

Standing the beer barrel upright, the master of ceremonies screwed in the stainless steel stopcock, and lifted it, with a bit of help, onto the open side of a donkey cart. He tested the flow of the liquid and after downing a half a tankard himself– just to test the quality – he attended to filling the array of beer mugs on the makeshift bar.

Not only was the air filled with the smell of the spit barbecue, but also mellow with catchy music being played by the trio of fiddle, bass and accordion. Lanterns had been strung around the newly cobbled square, suspended from the branches of the recently transplanted mature trees. Cut flowers floated below the huge cascading fountain located off-centre and out of the way of the traffic. The Taverna's tables spilled out onto the outdoor space rivalling the interior which invitingly beckoned the guests to enter and refresh themselves. In a convivial atmosphere people milled around and browsed the amenities on the perimeter of the square.

For Mr Rosenberg and his wife, the successful completion of Southcape was an occasion to celebrate in style, with five hundred invited guests to share their delight. It was early evening and a full moon was expected that night – quite auspicious they believed. Mr Rosenberg gazed with pride around the central space: it was the archetypal *placa, place* or *piazza* found in European villages where the new resident owners would be able to congregate and find company when they took up residence in their courtyard dwellings. Simon the architect - and he mustn't forget Nick the builder - had done a magnificent job of the design and construction. *Quite inspired*, people said, and it was so. Not only had they successfully created a unique living environment on a difficult city site, but they had the Atlas high-rise scheme overturned, and overcame any negative publicity which might have arisen from the unfortunate sabotage affair. Mr Rosenberg pulled a face at the memory, thanking his lucky stars that all had worked out so well in the end. Candice came up and kissed her father telling him how clever he had been in creating something quite unique. He beamed with pride.

The nightmare of the Atlas Company also passed fleetingly through Simon's mind as he surveyed the scene. Friends shook his hand and he was kissed on the cheek more times than he could remember with congratulations on his achievement. He had made a point of including other members of the architects' institute at the celebration as he felt that the whole profession could share the moment. They all were in the business of creating environments where people should feel at home and safe - Southcape's innovative city lifestyle was as good an example as any.

Nick slapped him on the back, 'Come on, pal, stop doing a mental inspection of the job – its all behind us now! Let's join the others at the table. I'll bring the beers.'

The buzz of conversation subsided as the master of ceremonies tapped a beer glass for Mr Rosenberg's speech. He was formally dressed in his striped suit and waistcoat and tie, and was helped onto the donkey cart so that he could be seen by all. Effusive in his praise, he peppered his speech with snippets of his brand of humour which those who knew him, associated with him. This was followed by the city's mayor, who also applauded the quality of Southcape's architecture:

'Such a fine addition to the inner city, of which other architects could take note!' he said. With the 'other architects' present, Simon considered the mayor's compliment a bit insensitive, but the occasion was his and the rest of the team, from Mr Rosenberg, to Nick as the builder, to his own staff, Rollo, Tim, Stefan and Jo.

Unexpectedly, the president of the institute of architects rose and called for quiet, wishing to make an announcement:

'May I have a moment, please – my committee and myself have been on a conducted tour around this brand new neighbourhood which has been most edifiying. Gone are the wellworn solutions to city housing, here we are experiencing something groundbreaking. We would like to congratulate Simon Duval who has shown a strong sense of how people want to live. We are proud to have him as a member of our profession. As a token of our commendation we would like to announce there will be a special award to Simon Duval Architect from the Institute for his really excellent design, faultlessly conceived and superbly executed.'

The clamour that followed the announcement was a prelude to the musicians' rendering of 'For he's a jolly good fellow', and Simon being hoisted on to the table to take a well-earned bow.

The mood of the gathering took on more momentum as he was lifted bodily over the heads of the crowd and marched off to the fountain, where he found himself on a ledge and leaning against the column of sculpted maidens in their flimsy flowing robes. Drenched to the skin, Simon was cajoled with good humour as he tried to satisfy the rowdy throng with an appropriate response, none of which was received with any decorum, but rather with a raucous rendition of, 'Why was he born so beautiful?'

The dancing and revelry continued into the night to the lively rhythms of the music trio. Simon eventually found the time to spend with Diane Chandler as promised who stayed much by his side after the fountain episode. She was back from London after appearing in shows in the West End. Her career in dancing blossomed from being back of the chorus line to being the understudy to the principal dancer. She had met Simon with mutual friends after one of the shows in London and thereafter they had spent quite a bit of time together. In many ways they were well suited, but Simon was not ready for a commitment beyond close friendship. The matter had rested there, that was, until her recent return to the Cape.

Desperately fond of him, Diane was protective to the point of being motherly. Towards the early hours she noted that not only Simon, but also their table companions were becoming a bit worse for wear. She confiscated his keys and fetched the Lancia. When Simon and Nick in a high state of inebriation insisted on seeing the new day dawn at Nick's apartment, Diane and Estrella drove them to the Nikolaides' waterfront house, but their boyish carousing had outstripped their capacity to stay awake.

Diane rose early from the sleeper couch on which she and Simon had spent the remainder of night at the Nikolaides' apartment. She dressed and he mumbled untelligibly as she kissed him on the forehead before commandeering his Lancia to drive herself back to her abode. A good excuse she reasoned, to see Simon again once he looked for his keys and found his first love was missing from the driveway.

12

The Cathedral project, as anticipated, occupied a large portion of Simon's working life. He delegated all other projects or outsourced them to smaller one-man practices and appointed an inhouse project manager to oversee the individual programmes. Sam de Bruyn was a highly experience construction man with an impressive portfolio of management in the industry. His greying hair at early middle age commanded the respect of the newly-fledged architects who had been favoured to work on Simon's outsourcing programme.

As the Cathedral took shape so the city councillors and the people began to take notice. It became the catalyst for urban renewal on the Cape Flats. The city budgeted to create an enormous landscaped setting for the Cathedral around which the traffic would circulate. There was to be an underpass to ease the crossing to the Cathedral for pedestrians. Simon was delighted with the enhancement of the surrounds as the newly created setting would add further stature to the aesthetic dignity of the Cathedral on its elevated podium.

A manufacturing yard had been set up on Cathedral site where the precast elements for the roof were subjected to rigorous testing. Nick had secured the contract for the precasting, giving Simon much peace of mind that quality control was strictly under Nick's watchful eye. The construction proceeded without too many hiccups, with the thick hollow walls of the egg-shaped plan rising pleasingly, providing a foretaste of the impressive scale of the complex.

The dedication of the Cathedral in its incomplete state was imminent, promising to become a significant event in the church calendar for that year. It was to be named, so the Archbishop had intimated, the Cathedral Church of St Francis of Assisi, as it was located over an ancient burial site for stray animals allocated by the city fathers at least one hundred odd years before. On the foundation stone itself, he noted with pride that the architect's name appeared in the last line under the Roman numerals recording the year of its laying.

The Archbishop's office sent out invitations to the stone-laying, a ceremony in keeping with the traditional blessing of the construction at an early stage. Earlier Simon was asked to provide a list of guests whom the Arch would invite and had no hesitation in including all his friends, past and present.

The day dawned bright and sunny, presaging goodwill for the ceremony due to take place mid-morning. There was to be a luncheon at the Archbishop's residence in one of the leafy suburbs of the City afterwards where an impressive array of dignitaries would be present: church men and women, captains of industry, politicians, the building contractors, professionals and Simon and Nick's friends. Despondently, Simon remembered his own family which had been reduced to two - himself and an aged aunt, his only surviving relative. She was too frail to attend.

A colourful procession in full church regalia, led by a boys' and girls' brass band from the Cape Flats preceded the main rituals. They processioned around the perimeter walls before entering the incomplete chancel - the place for the choir and clergy - which was beginning to take shape. The walls of the main body had reached full height, while the traceried ceiling, showing a blue sky through the patterned openings filtered light down over the chancel.

Nick was doing a great job, thought Simon comfortably to himself.

The hired organ installed for the occasion completed its introductory notes and the unroofed space rang out with the strong voices of the choir. Simon felt a sense of exhilaration as the high walls positively resonated superbly to the music. The acoustics had been tested on a model in the sound lab of the university before the final stages - but the real test would be when the Cathedral was completed. Mentally, he crossed his fingers as the success of failure of the main body as a place of worship depended very much on the reverberation levels being satisfactory, if not perfect for church music.

In his address the Archbishop was generous in his praise for the architect, and touched on the controversy which preceded the final choice of design. *Steady on, Arch*, thought Simon, *don't say more than you have to otherwise we could be getting into big trouble with a very disgruntled Ambassador and his daughter.*

All the special girlfriends in Simon's life, past and present, attended. The Velvet Club, he called them: Candice, Linda and Diane were turned out just as he expected, beautifully dressed and head-turning. They eyed one another secretly without a hint of acknowledgement. Diane and Candice went beyond competition for Simon's attention – they positively resented the other's presence. Linda on the other hand was still waiting for the overdue date which Simon used as a barter for the office in the Metrocity building, owned by her father. For the time being, with Diane occupying most of his off hours, he rather regretted his extravagant part of the deal. But there was no escaping – he owed her a date or an explanation. She hadn't forgotten either.

'Remember me, Mr Simon Duval, promiser of all good things and deliverer of none?' Linda was at his elbow.

'Wow, Linda, glad you came,' said Simon taking her hand.

'You mean lucky I came, after you have let me down over that promise.'

'Linda, how can I make up to you? I have been very, very busy, and am up to my eyebrows in this and another project¼ '

'You are up to your eyebrows in broken promises, Simon. I don't take to disappointments lightly. Just what other project are you talking about?'

Simon, breathed more easily as he recognised a shift in Linda's line of interrogation. As he began to explain how his days were spent in the office, she listened intently and began to thaw. In the end she even appeared impressed, congratulated him and pecked him on the cheek then him to devote her attention to another of her admirers who had just entered the room.

The Arch showing sharp powers of observation, rescued Simon from any further female harrassment.

'Simon, my boy, there is no mistaking your genius for designing the house of God, nor the fact that you have earthly worries, I see, with the opposite sex. Never mind, safety in numbers I say!' *Hmm*, mumbled Simon under his breath, *you have no idea how numbers in the Velvet Club have complicated the situation, good sir.*

Jo, Simon's right hand at the office, called him on his mobile.

'Simon, a most extraordinary call came from London. The Lord Mayor of London wants you to phone him. I have the number here so when you get back to the office I will get his office on the line for you.'

Instantly linking the call with Cathedral matters, Simon promptly forgot about the call, but on returning to office, Jo put through a second call from London.

'Mr Simon Duval, the architect?'

'Yes, good afternoon.'

'This is the office of the Lord Mayor,' said the voice, 'could you please hold for him? Thankyou.'

Simon sat down resting his feet on the desk. There was a short pause, then a confident English voice with obvious authority came on the line.

'Hullo, Mr Duval, Smith-Symonds here. Thankyou for taking this call. Mr Duval, the work you are doing in your country has attracted some attention. The Archbishop of Canterbury is particularly taken with what you are doing for the Cathedral project in your city and has recommended that you be shortlisted for the Earth Museum of Natural Disasters here in London.

'The Museum is going to have international donorship. If you are agreeable, you would be invited to submit a design for the Museum which will be located where the Millenium Dome used to stand, on the South Bank of the Thames. I take it that you know London?'

'Yes, I do. I don't know what to say, except¼ ' Simon gulped at the prospect, 'thank you for the honour of including me, Lord Mayor.'

'I take it that I can put you on the shortlist of participants then?'

Simon collected himself and was able to confirm his acceptance. The Lord Mayor's office was to courier the initial brief to him in the not too distant future, and there would be an opportunity to submit questions to the expert panel before the final brief was issued. Furthermore, he would be expected to attend various preliminary meetings in London and visit the site as frequently as he wished in preparation for his submission.

He put down the phone with his hands shaking uncontrollably, and flopped back into the chair. He stared disbelievingly into space for a full five minutes, then called Jo. There was loud applause from the staff when they heard the news. Simon spent the remainder of the day in a sort of mellow haze. However, until the courier had delivered the documents from the Lord Mayor's office for the Earth Museum of Natural Disasters, he immersed himself into completing the Cathedral project.

At last the couriered brief arrived, with a listing of all the other invited architects and their professional profiles.

Simon held his breath - it is an international line-up. Apart from himself he read aloud there were: Björn and Liv Seberg from Sweden, Ulrich Baumgarten from Germany, Roberto Severino from Italy, James Spencer from Scotland, Nahum Stern from Israel, Zahani Architects from Malaysia, Chegyan Dorje from Bhutan, Ryan Warner and Catherine Quaid from United States, Surendah Bahadur from India, Lars and Helga Norsman from Iceland. He pondered the importance of this opportunity for himself to participate in a highly competitive international field of some of the best architects in the world. The fact that Catherine Quaid's name was on the shortlist did not escape his notice.

Interesting, Simon concluded, apart from the geographical spread, the line up of the chosen few represented all the religions around the world. He wondered what the significance of this coincidence could be – or was it a coincidence? Was it because the religions were in effect the strongest agencies to manage the collective mindset of all the populations of the world on the pressing environmental issues facing the planet today?

He surfaced after a lengthy bout of speculation and looked at the scribble pad in front of him, covered with doodles which had no relevance at all. Then he called Jo to his office.

'Jo, you need to make flight and hotel reservations for me in London, please. The first session with the international shortlist is two weeks from now. I like that hotel in Bloomsbury where I usually stay, remember?"

*

Lord Mayor Smith-Symonds, with a token majoral chain around his neck, received the participant architects at an informal 'get-to-know-you' reception at Mansion House. The formal part of the programme would only begin the next day, starting early at the conference venue in the British Museum. Simon resided just around the corner at his favourite Bloomsbury hotel, so his choice of abode was fortuitously well placed and within walking distance.

The morning was shrouded in a swirling mist with the leaves of the London plane trees being swept into eddies along the ground. *Typical London day, but somehow the old buildings look better in this autumn light*, concluded Simon. He looked forward with some anticipation to seeing the British Museum which had been modernised with a complete makeover. He had known it as it was and he was not prepared for the breathtaking impact of the new translucent roof over the court which had transformed the old lady and given her a new lease on life. The diffused light from above played softly on the monotone neo-classical stonework. By contrast, the familiar central circular library with its darker colourful interior suited more studious pursuits and had become an inner sanctum within the larger space.

He saw Catherine Quaid in the distance and decided, at least for the time being, to give her a wide berth. She was immaculately turned out in a maroon Carducci two- piece and matching high heels. With her hair swept tightly back emphasising her fine profile she looked rather handsome, although a bit austere. The wide berth he gave her did not last for long. Catherine was suddenly at his side while he was peering up at the new roof, studiously avoiding her approach.

'Simon, how amazing, we're in another tournament together! How are you? I was delighted to see your name on the shortlist.'

'Hullo, Catherine. I am well thanks and you look ready for the tournament, as you call it. Actually this project is important to all those here, not just you and me,' said Simon trying to focus the conversation away from just the two of them.

'How reasonable you are Simon, and such a diplomat. Anyway, if you do get the commission, what will happen to your small practice in Cape Town? I mean you can't be everywhere, flying between the continents, can you?" she said insinuatingly.

He ignored the patronising flavour of the comment, and sallied forth: 'And what about your practice in Cape Town, doesn't the same principle apply to you?'

'Daddy has been transferred to the Secretariat of the

American Embassy in London and I will have a home here too. The Cape Town office just ticks over nicely without too much intervention on my side. A nice little nest-egg for safari trips and skiing holidays, actually. However, perhaps you would consider a merger, if either of us gets the commission for the Earth Museum so that we can share the commuting and run two lucrative practices. What do you say?'

Simon had anticipated exactly what Catherine was proposing and was ready with his response: 'I don't think that is going to work, Catherine. But thank you anyway. Our architecture is very different, not to mention our ethics.'

She accepted his last remark without a flinch. Instead she raised her chin proudly, getting in the last word: 'I am not so sure we are so different, Simon. Whatever makes you think we are?' Then turning, she nodded her goodbye and joined a group standing nearby.

It was not in Simon's nature to be quite so outspoken about personal differences, but he knew too much about Catherine, her outright plagiarism during the Cathedral competition and the culture she came from, which knew no bounds when it came to winning commissions. He felt uncomfortable about rattling her cage - somehow, somewhere he knew he would be facing retribution from that quarter.

The Earth Museum of Natural Disasters inaugural meeting got underway. The meeting co-chaired by two British architects, Ms. Evelyn Harrier and Mr John Jones, titled the 'Correspondents', introduced the so-called Initial Brief. The expert advisory panel was also introduced to the participants. It comprised project managers, representatives of the donor countries and experts in all fields of global ecology. The latter were atmospheric scientists, tectonic geologists, volcanic physicists, botanists, and writers on natural phenomena. Media technologists, otherwise known in the trade as 'techies', introduced the participants to the scope of the IT environment and interactive cyber technology which could influence the kind of architecture right at the conception stage.

'One thing must be made clear from the outset,' informed one of the Correspondents, 'you are not expected to know all about the technical nature of the exhibits in order to create the envelope into which the stories of natural disasters will be told. Your job will be the design of the envelope.' There was audible murmuring from the participants, sounding more like relief.

'The experts have produced a summary of natural disasters around the globe for which a considerable library of records exists around the world. These include hurricanes, floods, tsunamis, tidal waves, drought, earthquakes, volcano activity and the like. Sometimes there will be photographs or models, other times only statistics, so the field is wide, and the exhibits need to draw the spectator into the picture, educationally and entertainingly.'

The Correspondents drew attention to the timeline for the responses from the participants. All questions would be answered in writing regarding the brief, and then would become part of the Final Brief. Simon was in his element, although somewhat overawed by the prospect of distilling the highly detailed information-flow into the design process.

The Millenium Dome was to have been the flagship of the British millenium celebrations in the year 2000, but proved to be, if not a failure for the celebration itself, a financial albatross around the British government's neck.

It was dismantled and shipped elsewhere leaving a flat site around which the Thames snaked to form a prominence, almost a peninsula, known as the Blackwall Reach. The site lay almost exactly on 0° longitude, the Greenwich meridian.

The participants were flown by helicopter from the City to view the site and experience a sense of the place. From the air, features were pointed out as well as the connections from the north bank under the river. All aboard were favourably impressed - for something as important as the Earth Museum, the site was ideal. The Correspondents handed out three-sixty degree photographs of the site to the participants to augment their reference base while at their various places of work around the world.

Simon walked the entire length and breadth of the site, photographing the periphery extensively. Having the Greenwich meridian crossing the site – a geographical marker of global significance – was especially favourable. Across the Thames to the north bank the new glass tower blocks of the Isle of Dogs stood aloof as they disappeared and reappeared in the morning mist, as if to peep secretly at the activities on the opposite bank.

A trip on a river craft down river to the Thames Barrage followed the visit to the site. Simon noticed that the boatmen are old bargehands, who had grown up on the river and knew every inch of its course, and its moods. The Cockney skipper pointed out features of interest as the diesel engines rumbled in the bowels of the boat. Most of the river traffic comprised numerous heavily laden barges being hauled by lighter motorised craft.

By the time they reached the Barrage, the river had widened considerably. The Barrage itself stretched the entire breadth of the Thames, and an ominous reminder of the need to plan for potential disasters closer to home. The curved shiny metal hoods over the yellow hydraulic lifts reflected the colour of the sky and looked sculptural and appealing.

They were told by the boatmen that any flooding of portions of the City during an extreme climatic event would be a crisis of catastrophic proportions. The Barrage's role to prevent such a crisis developing and flooding the banks of the London waterfront was therefore crucial. Seeing the Barrage first hand was material proof that such a possibility was not being disregarded by those responsible.

They cruised close by the Barrage and Simon noted that the scale of the installation was immense, capable of withstanding a tidal surge of profound dimensions. It had happened before when the River Uck burst its banks and an overland flow occurred. Providing the means to prevent a recurrence was a tribute to the foresight of the City authority. The coincidence did not escape the candidates: they were not viewing an expensive meaningless installation, but staring at the distinct possibility of a future natural disaster with a direct associations with the planned Museum project they were being asked to design.

After a sumptuous lunch at Mansion House, the candidates dispersed. Simon took the express rail link to the airport. Airports were not high on his list of enjoyable places, but with a business class ticket courtesy of the Lord Mayor, the usual discomfort of the air travel could be eased. He boarded the 747 with his mind in a pleasing space, marshalling ideas which could be relevant to Earth Museum. One vivid recollection he had was the Dynamic Earth Centre in Edinburgh, a museum displaying the story of the planet from the 'big bang' to the present day. It highlighted the awesome forces which have shaped the natural environment, those which cannot be predicted or controlled and which generate a constant cycle of creation and destruction. *Definitely an interactive link with the Dynamic Earth Centre in Edinburgh could be developed as an indispensible part of the spectator experience*, he figured.

Thinking about the architecture itself, his mind was prompted to return again and again to the Taj Mahal, that piece of marble serenity, also situated on the bank of a river, the Jamuna, and on a flat site. How impressively its marble forms rose from its surrounds, changing with every light. And, then there were the behavioural aspects when natural disasters struck or were about to strike. Animals in particular anticipated extreme weather events, such as floods, better than people, and headed for the high ground. Humans seem to have lost this instinct, but through a sharpening awareness could develop their synchronicity with the other creatures for the sake of their own survival when natural disasters were about to happen.

The architecture of the Earth Museum needed to become an environment for depicting the destructive power of natural forces on the one hand, and on the other, ways of dealing with disaster events. Something positive had to flow for the average person from the experience of visiting the Museum.

Simon and Ulrich Baumgarten had met at the launch of the project and had not talked much about architecture – but finding that they enjoyed the same things in life, there was an immediate bond as though they had known one another for a much longer time.

Ulrich's own practice based in Stuttgart, was run like a well-oiled machine, staffed by some highly intellectual young architects, some still in training. They were voracious about everything happening in other design studios in the world, and sophisticated in their architectural preferences. Trends and fashion were not in their repertoire, and they believed implicitly in the direct evolution of architectural form and expression from the Bauhaus to the present day, otherwise the work was not mainstream. There was a distinct "inevitability" about good design, they argued, which simply implied that nothing should be added, such as ornament, which had no right to be there.

Simon related well to this philosophy and it wasn't long before the two chief architects were holding conversations telephonically and running up heavy phone bills. Then, not unexpectedly, came the proposal of marriage:

'Simon, jah? This is Ulrich. I have a proposition. We join our offices, jah, for the Museum, and create a beautiful architecture together. What is your answer, my *gutt freund*?'

Simon grinned to himself, as he had been expecting this proposition, but he also enjoyed Ulrich's use of basic English, always managing somehow to get the message across.

'Yes Ulrich, but first I must think about it.' said Simon cautiously. 'You have the edge on me, being in Europe, while my experience is confined to Africa.'

'Precisely, Simon, Africa is not¼ how would you say¼ shabby and an old girl like old Europe. Africa is full of life, waiting to have a chance, jah? We can do this together and make beautiful music, I know!'

Simon found the proposition appealing. He was not keen to expand his lean design office machine to cope with the enormous demands of a speculative project, like the Earth Museum at this stage, where there was no guarantee that he would "land the job" in the end. Although a handsome lump sum fee was being paid to the invited participants, it would be quickly soaked up in the overheads of his practice, and then hardly compensatingly.

Ulrich's offer was so persuasive that he accepted, and the Correspondents were duly notified that the two practices of Simon Duval and Ulrich Baumgarten would be submitting a joint proposal.

Weeks passed and the ideas of the two design studios for the Earth Museum reached a cross-road, a stage familiar in all architectural projects. Once there was agreement about the germ of the idea, things would become easier, then the embryonic design could be teased out for the full-blown reality. Simon and Ulrich needed to meet one-on-one to firm up the conception and steer the project in the right direction.

Simon flew to Stuttgart and was met at the airport by Ulrich's sister, Ingrid. She greeted him with Continental charm in perfect English, and almost as though he was a returning family member. It was a sunny spring day and the morning light played on her golden hair and her perfect complexion. *Hmm*, thought Simon remembering Diane, *this was not going to be easy*. They set off in an open black vintage Mercedes for the Baumgarten office downtown.

Ulrich's office was all that one would expect from a German architect – almost clinical, but with constant visual reminders of a devotion to the art of building. The walls displayed huge black and white photographs, even one showing Albert Speer's monumental concept for Berlin, which never saw the light of day, but was nevertheless still impressive. Furniture was minimalist, with some icons, such as the Charles Eames chairs in the reception area. In the studio state-of-the-art computer workstations in blue and grey were arranged in radial formation with low screens separating the operators. Well-tended potted plants landscaped the corners and were out of the way of the walking lanes. A feature was the generous private balcony overlooking the main platz of the city.

Ulrich came forward when they arrived, and offered a warm, welcoming handshake.

'Hope you had a good flight, mein freund?" Simon had no complaints and certainly none regarding the airport transfer service - Ingrid. She was as delightful to talk to as she looked and her expressive eyes made pleasing contact as she spoke. They sat down over filter coffee and pastries from the deli on the platz. Then Simon met the young architects around the office. There was no doubt that Ulrich ran a well-equipped machine, but one where art was not sacrificed on the altar of efficiency.

Ulrich showed Simon the view over the platz where dozens of pedestrians criss-crossed its patterned paving. Plane and linden trees defined the perimeter in front of the historic buildings, but a feature which caught Simon's eye was the simple structure in the centre, into which people were disappearing and occasionally re-appearing. *Probably the underground metro*, he decided.

The Earth Museum was soon under discussion between them. They sat across from one another with a pile of blank sheets of paper between them and a holder of felt tipped pens. Ulrich started the discussion:

'It seems to me, Simon, that we have to evolve our design philosophy, then develop the concept together, and then allocate sectors of the design for development.'

'And,' added Simon, 'we will need to keep a sharp eye on the relationship of the parts – the end product must be seamless.'

On those thoughts the discussion took off on a promising note setting the tone for the projects smooth-running future.

Since the inaugural meeting in London, Simon had given the design much thought, feeling that the site demanded prominent, yet simple architectural forms, with instant symbolic meaning for the spectator from the moment it is first seen.

'My first thoughts are, Ulrich, that there should be two parts to this Museum, which should be interdependent in the message they send out.

'Firstly, the planet's own idiosyncratic behaviour, leading to the disasters and their destruction of the earthly creatures and features, in so far as science has been able to identify and record them.

'Secondly, what would the earth have been like if there had not been any of the natural disasters as recorded? In this way the direct relationship of natural disasters to the evolution of life forms as we know them could be highlighted more strikingly. What is your view?'

Ulrich thought about this, then nodded in agreement. 'Also, the architectural form itself should suggest the message we are wanting to send out. But, please carry on,' he said.

Simon's view was that because the earth - a living organism, or Gaia according to the author Lovelock - was a sphere, the architecture could well be spherical and rotate, perhaps on a base or curvilinear podium.

He expanded on this idea: 'Let's take a huge sphere, a ball, say fifty metres in diameter with a fixed central shaft which rises from the depths of a podium. There could be branching galleries which support a tubular steel geodetic structure of the sphere. Fixed to that could be the stylised continental masses, cut out of huge sheets of embossed stainless steel, with the oceans in a steel mesh or something similar. This would then become the cladding in two finishes so that the continents and the oceans are easily legible.'

Simon continued: 'If the Earth's surface could show the main mountain ranges in relief, and other surface features like the tectonic faults, for example, down the west side of America and down the Rift valley in Africa, the planet would be depicted warts and all! Through the transparent mesh the viewer would be able to see into the centre of the Earth. Inside, the solid supporting shaft of the sphere could rise and feed into enclosed tunnels which could be exhibition spaces. Above, an extremely high tower penetrating the Sphere could beam out an advisory for any impending change to the planet's behaviour. It would symbolise the global communication network, like being one family.'

He sketched rapidly as he spoke. 'Two major components of the whole - the Sphere becomes the earth as we know it, with its scarrings and its present state of dynamic change, and the Podium which could depict the earth where natural disasters from recorded history have not taken place. For example, dinosaurs, which became extinct due to some catastrophic event, and the environment they roamed was different to that which we know. I suspect that the experts would have a wonderful time imagining what the evolved species would look like without the intervention of natural disasters,' concluded Simon with a grin.

Ulrich saw the potential of Simon's initial thoughts. He instinctively liked the less literal part housed in a Podium where the Earth without natural disasters could be presented, where the exhibits would have to rely on conjecture and scientific deduction. It seemed logical that Simon should design the earthlike Sphere and Ulrich's office, an appropriate architecture for the Podium, the two merging and complementing, one with the other.

Ingrid passed by their meeting numerous times and Simon felt distinctly distracted whenever the waft of her sophisticated perfume reached his nose. While Ulrich took a phone call, he wandered over to the balcony to view the platz. Again he noticed people coming and going from the bus stop-like structure in the centre.

Ingrid appeared by his side: 'What are you watching so intently, Simon?' she questioned.

'It's all the movement in and out of that flat-roofed building in the middle of the platz. I was wondering whether Stuttgart had an underground rail system.'

'Oh no, that. That is now a cheap hotel, but during the war it was the refuge of the Gestapo High Command. We can go down to see it if you like?'

They took the lift to the ground floor and strolled across to the centre of the platz. The entrance above ground was a modern structure, glass all around, with very little evidence of what lay beneath. Only the name of the hotel appeared in one of the glass panels.

On the first level down from the platz was a small space

with very basic furnishing and a desk to receive guests. 'Guttentag,' the gaunt pale-faced youth behind the desk uttered. They explained their curiosity to see the subterranean accommodation and were shown down a staircase into the bowels of the earth. Simon was astonished.

Off the main tunnel were bedrooms on either side, with the original airconditioning system still recycling the dank and rather stale air. The opportunity to escape the Allied bombing and be comfortably quartered must have pleased the original occupants, Simon figured. The link with the subterranean habitation of the termites which have survived many catastrophic natural disasters was obvious. *Survival was a powerful instinct for both man and insect giving rise to some of the world's most unusual structures, including this one,* he concluded philosophically, as they emerged into the daylight once more. The fact that the subterranean refuge sustained a low grade hotel in modern times was most enterprising.

For generations Ulrich and Ingrid's family had owned a farmhouse in the Black Forest. After the intense brainstorming over the Earth Museum, the end of the week arrived at last, presenting the opportunity for relaxation in the Forest and Simon was invited to join the Baumgartens. The prospect of enjoying his new found colleague's company, and of course that of his delightful sister, held great appeal for him.

They set off in the Baumgarten's vintage Mercedes with its tan leather seats and with the top down so that the fresh country air could be enjoyed and replace the smells of the city. The huge eight cylinder engine purred along the narrow treelined country roads, with the canopies of leaves reflecting like rapid psychodelic patterns across the car's long sleek mirror-like bodywork. The spring air was intoxicating as they rose higher and higher into the hills.

Approaching deep into the Black Forest up a winding road, they saw no other car. Suddenly the forest gave way to a clearing and there before them, edged by dense pines were grassed slopes surrounded by more dense forest. Traditional wooden farmhouses were dotted about, creating a sense of the kinship amongst the farmers. There was a 'rightness' about the architecture with the all-enclosing roofs, like mother hens sitting snugly over their eggs.

The Baumgarten farmhouse was one of the wooden Schwarzwald structures. Their aging friend and farmhand, Paula Klinghardt, greeted them at the door in her long, wrap-around apron. She wore Wellington boots and long striped socks, part of her standard dress for tending the cows. The scent of animals was strong throughout the house, but its cosy and refreshing authenticity down to the old photographs and embroidered texts on the walls was warm and inviting. The scrubbed wooden furniture was well worn, showing generations of use and teutonic housekeeping. The Baumgartens were attentive hosts and in no time Simon felt that he had been part of the family for longer than in fact was the case.

As the sun set, at Ingrid's instigation they walked out to stroll in the forest, with the noise of cow-bells constantly reminding them of the animals grazing in the clearings and on the grassed slopes. This for Simon, was a chance to regenerate, away from the demands of his practice in a distant place – a place to explore the other needs of the human condition, like recreation, which for a long time had escaped him. Taking leave of his new found friends and the place to get back to his distant practice thousands of kilometres away was going to be with a heavy heart.

After the restorative sojourn with the Baumgartens, Simon found himself still floating as he stepped onto the tarmac from the airplane in his home city. To meet him, Rollo had brought his old Volkswagen, which needed a push to get started. With the drive in the Baumgarten's Mercedes still in his mind, the contrast brought Simon down to earth with a bump.

The backlog on his desk on his return from Stuttgart amounted to a mound of paperwork, but with the agreement between the two practices now finalised he could focus on the architecture of the Earth Museum with a clear mind. Thinking of the project evoked images of Ingrid who was still very much on his thoughts - hopefully, those sentiments were being reciprocated.

His concentration was broken when the young architects in his office assembled at his studio door. They looked at him expectently and he waved them in to sit around his desk. *They are an impressive lot,* he thought, silently surveying their eagerness. He described to them the design concept he had agreed in his discussions with Ulrich, not leaving out a single detail so that a clear picture could be formed in their minds. He was handing the baton to them and wanted seed their ideas.

Rollo, whose design sensitivity had grown as the practice grew, articulated his thoughts about the design.

'Simon, the ideas you have brought back about the Museum are brilliant. There is a lot of scope with the concept. I have been thinking: since the globe for the Earth is located on Greenwich meridian, longitude 0° – amazing that it crosses the site – there is an opportunity to rotate the Sphere once every twenty-four hours to coincide with the its actual orientation – when the south side is in sunshine, that is daytime, the north side will be in shade, that is night time and so forth. So, the rotation of the Sphere will show what actually happens in fact. The central shaft with its the branch galleries could remain stationary within the Sphere.

'A great idea' said Simon encouragingly. 'But taking your suggestion further about rotating the Sphere: let's imagine longitude 0° is seen from the north - and the river - in the day time and other side of the globe, longitude 180° - Oz for example - seen at night? If we bring a light source onto the surface at night, then we can replicate the solar traverse over that part of the earth which is in sun, while in London it is night time. Can you imagine what that would look like from across the river? The site for the Earth Museum is so favourable, it allows us to do entertaining things, while at the same time it can be educational.'

'There is something else,' put in Rollo, 'I was reading about rainbow-like hologram surfaces, and what I have found is maybe something we can use. It says: "We only see a fraction of the light spectrum created by the sun. What we miss is dazzling. Hologram panels, making up a surface cladding with a special prism coating will be able to reflect and refract visible light frequencies. The spectacular array of glowing light and colour will change as the light source moves during the course of the day. Playing a laser beam across the surface after dark, brings out the real magic of the hologram, the invisible light will appear and the effect will be extraordinary.

He continued: 'The way we could use this is to emboss

the continents with hologram textures and the oceans in a see-through stainless steel mesh. Sun and laser light will create amazng effects both day at night.'

Simon absorbed the possibilities silently for the moment – Rollo was coming up with some pretty impressive refinements for the design concept.

'That's an inspirational idea,' he said, 'in fact, let's try modelling up the entire concept now, and play with the light sources, daylight and laser, and let's test the physics. Also to check out the textures, as you suggest. Maybe they will work maybe not, but I have a sneaking suspicion that we are on to something special. Oh, then don't ignore Ulrich's podium – that needs to be included in the overall scheme of things. Meantime I'll let him know what we are working on, and ask him to sketch out some concepts we can include in a model.'

Thousands of kilometres away, intent on their own imposed standard of excellence, Ulrich's architects were rigorously exploring numerous options for the Podium, and beginning to eliminate the less likely ones. He is full of praise for what Simon's office had suggested for the Earth Sphere, which, in turn, provided more impetus to their ideas. It was as though through their interdependence both offices were striving for an even greater degree of excellence.

The scale of the Podium's above and below ground had to be impressive, after all it was to house vast halls of diaramas. The idea of subterranean levels, where the substrata of the earth could be exposed to view and possibly the organisms which inhabit below-ground conditions was also being investigated. Another feature could be a tunnel extending up to the Thames terminating in a glass bubble where the submarine life of the river along one side wall could be viewed, but the relevance of this to the brief was still open to question.

For the Podium to have its own identity, his architects were proposing a free form of three-storeys above ground, fragmented like a giant jigsaw puzzle with its portions shaped to match the Gondwanaland continental clustering. The crevasses between the continents would become light wells into the interior. Sunken into the vast top deck would be an amphitheatre with slide-way roof for large audiences to view media presentations on an IMAX screen. An astonomical observatory and astrological installations, the latter like the Janta Mantas found in India, clad possibly in titanium, and expressed in a deconstructivist design language would to rise partially above the deck. Four levels below ground would be for parking and would contain the station link with the underground rail system. The central shaft of the Sphere would rise from the lowest level of the Podium, with multiple elevators connecting with all the exhibition halls and galleries.

Ulrich offered to send on these ideas electronically for Simon's team to model. It seemed to both of them that the teamwork was paying off.

Architects Duval and Baumgarten managed the deadline for submissions for their entry. Drawings, video reconstructions and a model occupied an enormous customised container which was couriered to the Correspondents in London just on time.

They both realised that the worst time in any competition programme was waiting for the outcome. They expected news within a month, however, after many weeks, the scheduled announcement of the appointment for the Earth Museum was yet again delayed. Simon's enquiries provided no explanation for the delayed announcement, until one morning on the phone to the office of the Correspondents, the secretary who remembered him from the inaugural meeting spilt the beans.

'Yes, Mr Duval, everyone wants to know what is causing the delay. I am afraid I know very little about the deliberations that take place behind closed doors, but I do type the minutes. If you promise not to let on I'll tell you what seems to be the reason.'

'Well, that would be most welcome, and I promise not to disclose any sources whatsoever,' said Simon appreciatively.

'The minutes of the past three meetings record that there is a single vote of dissent by a representative of one of the donor countries who is on the jury. This influential person has disagreed with the panel's choice – I can't tell you who it is but the panel's choice has to be unanimous. I am sorry this has delayed the announcement of the successful architectural practice. Does that help, Mr Duval?'

'Well, yes it does, thankyou,' said Simon distractedly considering this latest piece of information. The idea of a jury member interfering with the outcome had a familiar resonance? Could it mean that he and Ulrich were the practice over which there remained a dispute?

Six months after the inaugural meeting for the Earth Museum of Natural Disasters, the delayed of the announcement of the successful three finalists was imminent. With all the hype and publicity preceding the announcement, public curiosity was bristling with impatience.

For the finalists it was a nail-biting wait, however, the moment of truth was at hand. After the first round there were three known finalists, all of whom had formed consortia: Spencer and Seberg, Stern and Quaid, and Duval and Baumgarten. During the countdown to the announcement of the panel's final choice, the tabloids ran front page headlines with photographs of the three finalists' models and the London bookies had a field day. The odds were lowest on the entry of Stern and Quaid.

Eventually, on prime time world radio and on the international television networks, Simon and Ulrich's imaginative and innovative rotating globe on its Gondwanaland podium was judged the winner. Their jubilation knew no bounds, but from then on their lives become public property. Sudden notoriety thrust them onto the front pages of the newspapers and they were booked to appear as guests on both the popular and the more erudite talkshows on radio and television. It seemed that the public couldn't get enough of the story. Much as though he enjoyed all the excitement, for Simon there remained one nagging thought, buried deep in the recesses of his mind – *Ms Quaid was not going to like this one bit.* He thought of the Velvet Club, that imagined sorority who were a challenge individually and collectively.

To be at the actual scene of the project during the development phase, Simon figured that there would be many working trips to London. The novelty of spending nights in a hotel would soon wear off. He concluded a lease of an apartment on the northern bank of the Thames overlooking the site. There was something congruous about his choice of abode he realised - after all, didn't Sir Christopher Wren do the same during the construction of

St Pauls - locate his quarters opposite the building site? It was an appealing solution. Ulrich was to be his guest until the TV shows were over. In between time they spend many daytime hours researching ideas in London's almost uncountable galleries and museums.

As winners of perhaps the most prestigious architectural commission of the decade, TV host, Michael Flanagan, invited the winning pair to appear together on his talk show. The two architects were being hounded by women's magazines and tabloids all wanting to scratch around for some romantic titbits they could pass on to their readers. So, they are hot news, and in fact celebrities, and were not about to be released to their respective countries until the media hounds had finished with their pickings.

Michael Flanagan's television show was a focus on popularising more celebral spheres of culture, architecture being only one. The hour-long slot on prime time was meant to be both entertaining and educational, so it was therefore a surprise when once the introductions were over, Flanagan, in his mild Irish tongue, threw his guests what appeared to be a serious curved ball.

'Now as the men of the moment, can you explain to our viewers: why has your undoubted success been marred by scandal in the corridors of power, so to speak?' Simon looked at Ulrich for help, but none was forthcoming.

'Gentlemen,' he went on, 'here is a short paragraph in one of our most illustrious dailies, reporting that the choice of architects for the Earth Museum is, as we speak, being contested behind closed doors.'

Flanagan handed them the article and the camera picked up the text on the screen for the viewers, and continued to talk:

'It seems that the choice has not been unanimous after all. But let me immediately add that nothing can demean your wonderful architectural concept which will hopefully rise without further controversy on the Millenium site. Viewers have been phoning in and emailing the Corporation in their admiration of what will be a great contribution to London's architectural stock.'

Simon and Ulrich were unable to enlighten the viewers other than to express their astonishment and that nothing about the controversy had been conveyed to them by the organisers, and as far as they were concerned, that was that.

Back in the privacy of the apartment, Simon contacted the Lord Mayor's secretary about the alleged discord amongst the organisers. His good fortune was in. Ms Goodenough, a spinster who had taken a shine to him, was standing in for the tightlipped Mr Thorneycroft.

'I am not sure I should be telling you anything you should not know already, Mr Duval. But since you ask, frenetic discussions have been taking place behind closed doors. I have seen ambassadors of the donor countries going in and coming out. The American ambassador – it's best I don't disclose his name – has been the most frequent visitor to the Lord Mayor in his chambers.'

'You mean Ambassador Quaid¼ ?'

'Yes, I believe so, Mr Duval,' she agreed reluctantly, 'you see, America is one of the major donor countries to the project. That is really all I can tell you. I am sorry. But let me add my voice: in choosing your proposal with the Stuttgart architect I believe the panel were absolutely right. There I have said it.'

'Thankyou, and thankyou again, Ms Goodenough,' Simon said sincerely.

'You are welcome, Mr Duval, and good luck,' she added cheerily, with her voice ending on a high note.

Stunned with the revelation, Simon returned the receiver to its hook, his mind racing.

He shook his head in disbelief: Could it be that they would not get the project after all, in which case, payback time for his frank remarks to Catherine have come earlier than he'd have expected? Ulrich waited patiently to hear the news, and could see from Simon's body language there had been a disturbing news.

'Ulrich, my friend, you will not believe what I have been told, which is enough to hang a person. My conclusion is that it is the American ambassador has put the cat amongst the pigeons at the Lord Mayor's office. America is one of the major donor countries. He has got to be the cause of that delay over the panel's choice at the outset, you remember? He is Catherine Quaid's father, recently transferred to the American embassy in London, having done his stint in Cape Town. She, as you know, was one of the three finalists architects for the Earth Museum, and since she didn't get the commission with the Israeli architect, Stern, her father is trying to get the panel's choice – that's us! – overturned!'

Ulrich shook his head in complete disbelief. 'Trust the Americans,' he offered cynically, 'they believe the dollar buys them the right to rule the world. But the panel's choice has been made public and there is no cheap way out for the Lord Mayor now, Simon. There could be a string of litigation claims for damages - even the bookies who have paid out big amounts of money to the winners who forecast the outcome. I wouldn't want to be in his shoes.'

'Let me explain my history with Catherine Quaid: She

set up shop in Cape Town when her father was deployed there. She ran against me in the Cathedral competition and lost. Her father dangled a carrot in front of the Archbishop's eyes in an attempt to get them to change their choice – my concept! She cheated and was guilty of industrial espionage in my office, which was provable. The Arch, of course, didn't like that one bit and thereafter she had no chance. I knew that somewhere down the line, I would be paying not only for winning, but for exposing her deceit, and here it is. She put her father up to this. Through the Quaid connections in the US, he obviously has influence back there in the States and is trying to secure a place for Catherine on the project.'

What appalled them both was the lengths to which humans would go to avenge past grievances, or to avoid the impression of having failed. Their next step was a letter hand delivered to the Lord Mayor's office referring to the paragraph in the London daily. They had, they wrote, come across reference to a controversy over the Earth Museum appointment, and would like to have confirmation of what exactly the position was. Two days later, a letter in response arrived from Mr Thorneycroft confirming their appointment as "the architects jointly responsible for the design, and successful implementation of the International Earth Museum for Natural Disasters". It stated that there should be no further confusion about their appointment.

Now that they could celebrate without any doubt, the two winning architects had to admit that their model itself was a winner, much credit to their combined staff who put in many late hours to complete it in the Stuttgart office.

At a much publicised ceremony at Mansion House, they were handed a cheque for £1m as an advance on their fees to bring the project into being. Simon's face was all over the newspapers, as the successful architect from Africa – and the first from that continent to win in a high profile international architectural competition. He even received proposals of marriage on email from around the globe.

As architects they were staring at fame and launched firmly onto the international stage. But it was time to lie low, away from the media, and get back to the simple life: where better than in the Black Forest at the Schwarzwald farmhouse of the Baumgartens? There were only a few formalities from which they could not escape before that beguiling prospect could be turned into a reality.

Buoyed by Mr Thorneycroft's letter and £1million in the bank, Simon and Ulrich treated themselves to a chartered flight from London Airport, destination Stuttgart. As the plane left the airstrip it flew over the Earth Museum site. Simon looked down and considered the future: knowing the track record of Catherine Quaid, he expected that their paths would one day cross again. He was convinced that after the two, maybe three failed episodes when she had tried to outsmart him, she regarded him as her arch rival, if not her enemy Number One.

The black Mercedes manouvred with elegant class along the narrow country road as they drove to the town of Todtnauberg on the edge of the Black Forest. Ulrich was delayed on business in Ulm and he and his wife, Helga, would join Ingrid and Simon in due course. She drove the vintage car with familiarity and confidence, while Simon reclined in the passenger seat. He looked silently at her perfect profile, and felt he was in a free-fall over her, the relationship having grown warm between them.

'Penny for your thoughts, Simon,' she prompted, snatching a sidelong glance at him.

'I was thinking, that I might hire you as my chauffeur back home,' he teased, watching for her reaction.

'That would depend on what there is in it for me, sir.'

'Well, perhaps I could offer to buy you a house, a car – you know all things which are closest to a girl's heart.'

'Are you sure you know enough about a girl's heart?' she said smiling, taking her eyes off the road for a brief moment and looking steadily at him.

'That is what I want to find out this weekend.'

There was a growing awareness between them that their's was not going to be just another relationship. The chemistry was for real.

As on previous occasions, Paula greeted them at the door with two black labradors suddenly making their appearance and wagging their pleasure at the arrivals.

The day wore on and it was evening before Ulrich and Helga joined them in time for one of Paula's solid Alpine-style evening meals. They lingered over the gluwein while sitting around the ceramic tiled central oven to keep warm before a meal at the sturdy old oak table. Paula's cuisine was peasantlike and nourishing, ideal for the cold autumn in the high altitude of the Black Forest. It was not long before they all retired, Simon finding himself in an attic room with wooden panel walls, grey with age. He could hear the cows on the ground floor and looking down through the floor cracks he could see the lines of their backs as they swayed complacently back and forth. There was none of the usual conventional bedding - the duvet on the wide bed was unlike anything he has slept under before. It was an enormous cushion of pure down under which to escape the world until morning. In no time his weary body succumbed to the warmth and the gluwein.

In the morning Ingrid rose first, and busied herself in the kitchen. She put on the coffee and waited for the aroma to permeate the house through the old wooden walls and floors. A thick mist outside resembled a white-out with visibility down to a few metres. Paula burst in through the outside door, her cheeks flushed pink from the cold. She had been up since before light to take the cows out to pasture.

Ulrich and Inga arrived before the mist had risen so the four played mahjong until around mid-morning until it cleared and time for a walk in the Forest to look for mushrooms and perhaps with luck, truffles. They took the winding trail up the grassed slopes and entered the dank environment of the pine forest with its canopy of the trees screening out the light from the pale sky. The forest floor was thickly littered with pine needles, where occasionally mushrooms appeared for the taking. They foraged in pairs, and when Simon next looked up, he and Ingrid had separated from the others, but they had agreed to meet at the clearing. By then the sky had cleared.

They came across a small chapel with Gothic features, complete with belfry over the entrance. It seemed auspicious for the way Simon felt at that moment.

'Shall we find a priest?' Simon said straightfaced, watching for Ingrid's reaction.

'Oh, no, Simon Duval, there are still a whole lot of rituals to courtship – rites of passage – no girl worth her salt would skip any of them, just because there is a cute chapel.' He grinned, liking her sharp wit.

From the clearing on the edge of the forest, the view towards the south was spectacular. The snow-capped peaks of the Alps were clearly visible after the morning mist lifted. They sat down on a rug in the gentle sunshine. For what seemed a long time Simon looked at Ingrid and she at him. Placing his hand on her shoulder, he drew her towards him. Their lips touched softly, and both felt the response they had each hoped for. He kissed her meaningfully, so that she had no doubt that he was falling in love with her. They pulled away and look grinningly at each other, saying nothing as their eyes said it all.

The moment was interrupted by the arrival of Ulrich and Helga, who needed no explanation about the chemistry they were observing. Ulrich believed he could not ask for a better match for his sister.

With the Cathedral of St Francis in Cape Town completed and finally dedicated to the glory of God, Simon could at last devote more time to the Earth Museum of Natural Disasters in London. Work had proceeded apace in his practice, and his staff had expanded with the intake of two more fledgling architects, Kevin and Sonya.

For the best part of a year, Simon and Ulrich visited the Earth Museum site where construction was underway in earnest. They had agreed to combine their visits there where typically many things, often the minutiae of the design, needed first hand negotiation between them. In any event they enjoyed sharing the great promise of their joint design as it rose before their eyes.

The experts advising on the content of the displays and the museum stylists had produced scale models of their exhibits, which were being transformed into drawings for the construction team on site. The contractors, a large international consortium, were generally complimentary about the design and the way things are going.

The prominence of the site next to the Thames attracted a lot of interest from the tourist traffic on the river. Construction had began first with a deep hole in the ground for the subterranean levels of the Podium. A year later the sheer scale of the Sphere, the Earth structure, stood proudly with the branching galleries suspended off the central shaft already in place. The fifty metre spherical geodetic frame was only a promise of what was to come.

Destined to receive displays depicting a planet and earth forms unravaged by recorded natural disasters, the Podium had a life of its own, inspiring natural scientists and the display specialists into new heights of creativity with the use of cutting edge electronic displays. The viewers would be enjoying groundbreaking virtual experiences. Above ground level the Podium was fragmented into shapes depicting Gondwanaland and did indeed look like a giant jigsaw puzzle. Already construction-workers were busy in the large gaping hole in the deck for the amphitheatre with its slide-way roof for large audiences and for media presentations on an IMAX screen.

For the public, previews of the creative work of the exhibition consultants were being flighted regularly on television, with visuals anticipating the finished components of the building. An interesting feature was the lookout deck at the top of the Earth Sphere at the North Pole.

There were some setbacks. Throughout the year the contractors recorded many heavy raindays which were delaying their completion schedule. The site was being pumped through all twenty-four hours of the day to keep it drained – not easy under the circumstances as the Thames swelled constantly to the rim of the Thames wharfside.

The Barrage was doing its job, holding back the sea in Thames estuary, and was preventing the flooding of much of London's low-lying water frontages. There were fears that the frequency of dangerously high tides due climate change were on the increase from once a century to once in a decade, which only justified the need for the Barrage. For the time being, or so the experts were assuring the public, there was no need for concern - in hydraulic terms an even greater water body could be detained if the Barrage was raised to its ultimate limit. But that peace of mind was about to be tested.

Ulrich picked up the buzzing of his mobile phone. It is the foreman's office. A voice spoke rapidly and urgently:

'Sir, an emergency alert has been sent out on the radio, the Thames Barrage has breached and a tidal flood is expected to reach Greenwich in five minutes. The foreman says that all site personnel must please evacuate to the roof of the Podium now¼ '

Without further warning Ulrich and Simon could already hear the sound of rushing water and, to their horror saw a cascade of brown slush shooting through an opening in far corner of the subterranean level where they were standing.

'The river must have already burst the banks of the site and reached the building,' yelled Simon above the mounting roar.

They raced to the stairwell but were stopped in their tracks by waves of brown water impeding their path and rapidly filling the subterranean void. Through its sheer force, the growing torrent made escape impossible. In their forced separation it was each man for himself. Simon clung to a floating wooden workbench with the turbulent water rising rapidly higher and higher and closing the gap between floor and ceiling. He caught sight of Ulrich swimming frantically towards the nearest stairwell and watched in horror as its opening disappeared below water level. Helpless in a vast dark concrete receptacle his only means of survival was a floating bench.

Simon forced himself to recover his calm and not to surrender to his predicament. Instinctively he knew that, caught in an overpowering force, the victim's best chance of survival was not to waste energy in a futile struggle. He consciously willed himself to comply, through turning his thoughts to Ingrid - *and what of Ulrich, did he make it in time?*

Miraculously, Ulrich was swept through the door of the stairwell, recovered his footing and raced up to the roof two steps at a time with the water level rising rapidly behind him. He was helped onto the deck while teems of site workers emerged from the flooding vertical shafts, and shook themselves off like wet dogs. They huddled together and took stock.

From the upstream surge of the tide, the Thames had inundated the sites surrounding the unfinished Earth Museum, which stood as if it were an island in a brown sea. *Global warming had blurred the line between man-made disasters and natural disasters,* Ulrich concluded. The cause of the dramatic rise of the Thames would no doubt be the subject of continual investigations and the consequences talked about endlessly for generations to come. Why the Barrage had failed would be the question everyone wanted to have the answer to. *Meantime, where was Simon?*

Simon hugged his ship of mercy and was swirled back and forth in the flooding Podium. In his growing exhaustion he pleaded for the mercy of a higher power to rescue him. He reminded himself of Isambard Kingdom Brunel, the Victorian engineer, who was the first to tunnel under the Thames at Greenwich to connect the north and south banks for pedestrians and horses to use. Brunel's methods were archaic by today's methods - he left no doubt that he was a genius, a man before his time, who was often being let down by the limited engineering knowledge and technology of the times. Simon remembered that during Brunel's tunnel construction, the wall breached allowing the river to burst in to fill the void at great speed. *Today we have the means but still we can't stop disasters like this one,* Simon shouted out loud to himself.

Again, Brunel's extraordinary confidence in his abilities sometimes outstripped the realities of the times. After the initial flooding of the Thames tunnel and after working on the tunnel face had resumed, Brunel resolved to celebrate by holding a banquet in the reclaimed workings. Hung with crimson drapery and lit by gas candelabra, the tunnel was an impressive setting for the fifty-odd select guests and the one hundred and twenty miners who feasted not far away. They dined to the accompaniment of the Coldstream Guards. The celebration was premature as disaster struck again with renewed determination to scupper the project. Brunel nearly lost his life. Caught in the flooding of the tunnel, he escaped only by his cool capacity not to panic. Somehow this thought buoyed Simon's hopes of recovery. *What chutzpah, Brunel, let's hope my luck holds too,* he muttered to himself between his uncontrollable shivers.

The maelstrom propelled by the incoming flood forced him and his makeshift life raft towards a vertical shaft. A voice shouted down the shaft interrupting his numbing mind. He looked up to see the construction foreman peering down from above. Help was on its way. Words of encouragement brought tears of relief to his eyes.

A helpline like a lasso was lowered and with extreme effort he treaded water and wriggled his body into it. His limbs ached from the cold water and rope in his hands was the most welcome gift he could have wished for. The emotion of being lifted away from a watery grave was one of merciful relief. Simon thanked his guardian angels - all of them.

The sight of the river from the deck is a shock. The Blackwall Reach around the heel of the Museum site had grown to twice its normal width with the buildings on the opposite bank surrounded by life-threatening eddies. Miraculously, the Museum structure had so far resisted the force of the flood and outwardly, appeared undamaged. Police helicopters circled overhead, no doubt recording images of the swollen river for recovery and rescue operations - and the huge insurance claims that would certainly follow.

Simon stood dazed and drenched until he was offered a blanket and guided to the emergency station for medical attention. There he found Ulrich, who is already changed and dry and looking decidedly glad to see his colleague alive. Their escape with only cuts and bruises was a miracle.

'A bit too close for comfort, mein freund, jah?' Ulrich said, mustering a grin and giving Simon a friendly hug.

'You can say that again,' quipped Simon, surprised at his own recovery, 'but this natural disaster couldn't wait for us first to complete the Museum! It has got to be one of the exhibits in the Museum depicting all the drama that goes with it. Not to forget the sight of the human rats on the deck, after their rescue from a watery end!'

The story was breaking news on radio and all the international TV channels interrupted the normal programmes with live visuals taken mostly from the air. In Stuttgart, Ingrid and Helga watched the interviews with the survivors and heard the eye witness accounts, but Simon and Ulrich didn't feature. After many desperate enquiries, they booked seats on the earliest flight out to London.

"A New Age architectural icon has arisen on the Thames South Bank at Greenwich. In its architectural excellence it represents a growing consciousness about our habitat, planet earth and its ability to determine the destiny of all things. For the Earth Museum of Natural Disasters, the architects have conceived a sphere, depicting land masses and oceans as we know them, inside which we can perambulate and see dramatic linear displays. Relying on the light of day and laser light at night, the use of the hologram texture of the continents uses the full colour spectrum with great subtlety and effect. It is a true monument to our Earth Mother. Equally inspired is the curvilinear Podium, configured in the shapes of Gondwanaland with a modern astronomical observatory and historic astrological installations occupying parts of the vast upper deck.

People from around the world will find this experiential building entertaining and educational, signifying the close collaboration between the architects, the museum specialists and the formidable array of experts who advised on the exhibits – not to forget the building contractors. The Museum deserves the highest acclaim from the international community for its clarity in presenting the environmental forces around us over which we have limited control."

This piece written by the architectural correspondent appeared in The Times the day before the grand opening of the Earth Museum for Natural Disasters – London, England, Planet Earth - extolling its worth as an architectural statement and its effective environmental message. It was also announced that a scale model of the Earth Museum as well as the architects' drawings would be on display at the Victoria and Albert Architecture Gallery, where the RIBA's own collection recently found a permanent home.

Commencing late afternoon, the official opening of the Earth Museum was managed with the usual aplomb and ceremony for which the British were famous. The somewhat lofty pitch of the Lord Mayor Smith-Symonds's voice was busy addressing the huge gathering of dignitaries, amongst whom were visiting monarchs, prime ministers and presidents, professionals and the general public. Most of the latter had queued overnight to be present at the inauguration day. The publicity had been extensive throughout the construction period, revving up to a pitch towards the day of opening.

Due to the breaching of the Thames Barrage, and the drama that ensued, the world's attention was focussed on the project. The near fatal episode involving the architects and others caught up in the flood waters, filled the pages of the popular press.

Looking around him during the precedings, Simon was gratified that the environmental lobbies have given their blessings, particularly Green Peace whose banners fluttered pleasingly around the Podium. It was an endorsement of the complex as a valuable educational environment in keeping with that green movement's own initiatives.

Seated on the deck, the large gathering began to shift restlessly on their seats as the amplified voice of the Lord Mayor droned on, thanking all the donor countries and all those involved with the project from its inception. All the donor countries were represented by top level officials.

As the light of day began to dim, a helicopter fly-past saluting the occasion with trailing flags of all the donor countries, brought a welcome end to the speeches. The combined roar of the flailing rotor blades roused the gathering from their induced torpor and was enough to raise the dead.

Simon and Ulrich, with Ingrid and Helga, were in seats designated for important people. Towards the close, the master of ceremonies called Simon and Ulrich to the rostrum, where to much applause, the Lord Mayor welcomed them with a handshake. Warming magnanimously to the occasion the President of the Royal Institute of British Architects addressed the gathering to end the proceedings:

'Throughout the world,' he said, 'this project, the Earth Museum of Natural Disasters, has achieved recognition as an architectural achievement of considerable excellence. Its siting on the Greenwich meridian, the international date line, symbolically strengthens the geographical interdependency between the continents around the world, and thus promotes a collective world view. Natural disasters have killed millions of people from time immemorial, and in the exhibits housed in these immense structures we are reminded that we are at the mercy of the unstoppable forces of Nature. You will recall that the Museum construction itself was tested by a natural disaster when the Thames flooded the site two years ago with the loss of two lives. It stood the test and progressed to become the fine architectural landmark you see around you.

'On behalf of various affiliated institutes of the RIBA throughout the world, I have the honour to present this joint architectural and environmental award to the architects Simon Duval and Ulrich Baumgarten, in recognition of the excellence of their architectural concept which so effectively presents the true nature of our planet in all its moods.'

A stylised scale model of the Museum (a sort of architectural Oscar), crafted in polished stainless steel, was handed to each architect by the Minister of Arts and Culture followed by handshakes all round and prolonged applause from the gathering. Ingrid and Helga looked admiringly at their partners, Simon and Ulrich, who, clutching their 'Oscars', waved to the crowd as they left the rostrum.

As if to launch the gathering into party mode, arrows of light shot into the early night sky, taking everyone by surprise. Climaxing in spectacular cascades of phosphorescent fireballs, volleys of rockets whooshed skywards in rapid succession, lighting up the Podium deck and the Earth sphere as if it were daylight. At that moment the Lord Mayor threw the switch which started the Earth's quiet, and almost imperceptible rotation. Designed with an outer skin which revolved around the internal structure, with a play of ambient evening light on the Earth's hologram cladding, the sight was awesome, even more so with the laser beams creating moving shafts of light across the darkening sky, like the antlers of a giant insect feeling its way.

Guests were invited to follow the appointed guides to view the Earth sphere and the Podium from within. The entry to the galleries in the Earth sphere, then in its slow rotation to a twenty-four hour cycle, was by a large bank of elevators located at the Podium deck, while visitors entered the Podium through banks of escalators into the vast subterranean body.

It was like entering into other realms: in the Earth Sphere the planet realistically depicted in sight and sound. Huge diaramas illustrated it's idiosyncratic behaviour, which had led to disasters and the extinction and destruction of the earthly creatures and features. And, in the Podium, a world of scientific make-believe, displaying what the earth and its creatures would possibly have been like if there had not been any of the known natural disasters over eons of time. The scientists had excelled themselves and the display specialists had succeeded in creating an environment of awesome evocation.

Simon led their party to the Earth Sphere. They peered up the central shaft where glass-walled elevators clung to the sides of a wide drum, carrying the visitors to the topmost level and the North Pole viewing deck. Through the use of colour, a transect from the Earth's crust in cool blues and greens to its inner core in orange and red heightened the experience as the elevators shuttled up and down. The galleries, extending like branches of a tree from the central shaft, had revolving displays which changed electonically to match the twenty-four hour revolution of the Earth.

From the viewing deck at the North Pole the lights of London created a glow over the city, The Gondwanaland configuration of the Podium could be seen below them with the crevasses separating the continents were bathed in a blue light depicting the oceans as they once were in geological time.

Simon felt overwhelmed with the emotional charge of the moment. He had come a long way from his first assignment as an architect. *But where to from here?* he wondered. He had spent so much time dealing with the hyped events around the Earth Museum of Natural Disasters, it had almost become his addiction. It would be hard to turn away from the project and repeat the experience with another. When projects were completed there was usually a sense of emptiness for the architect, needing to be filled by new challenges.

During one of his visits to London Simon had received a call from the Moroccan embassy, inviting him to meet with the Moroccan ambassador whenever he was next in the City to discuss another possible project. As the moment was opportune, he sought out the ambassador at the Lord Mayor's reception which followed the launch of the Earth Museum, to find out what Morocco might have in store for him.

Chapter Four

The interiors of the Moroccan embassy in London were like a page from a travel book on Morocco itself, and lavishly embellished with stuccowork, heavy drapes and gold trimmings, showing the nation's love of colour and rich detailing. Simon was first ushered through endless lobbies by the secretary and who then departed silently after the formal introductions were concluded.

The Moroccan Ambassador, Monsieur Hassan al-Moulay, related key points of recent Moroccan history to Simon over tea, poured from a tap in a tiered and elaborately decorated ceramic tea urn.

'The Moroccan king,' Monsieur al-Moulay proceeded to tell Simon, 'was so impressed with the architecture of the Earth Museum, he extended an invitation to you to visit Rabat to meet with his representatives about a project he has in mind for the Western Sahara territory.'

The prospect of working in Morocco conjured up visions of Arabian nights, kasbahs and souqs. *Utterly exotic*, thought Simon, as he listened approvingly to ambassador outlining the project.

As the ambassador spoke, Simon marshalled his thoughts about what he had read in preparation for that meeting: The Western Sahara Desert was evacuated by Spain in 1975, when Morocco and Mauritania both raised claims to the sparsely populated desert territory. Soon Morocco asserted its interests in the territory but met with resistance from a rebel guerilla group. Twenty years later, the King of Morocco orchestrated a Green March and led over three hundred thousand of his countrymen into the Western Sahara to stake Morocco's historical claims to the territory. 'The March', as it became known, was followed by troops sent in to stamp out resistance. To hamper the rebels' movements, the Moroccan government erected a sand wall, one and a half thousand kilometres long, demonstrating that Rabat was determined to maintain the upper hand.

Although formal, the ambassador was an old hand at bridging the cultural divide and made Simon feel welcome and at ease. The more he heard the more he warmed to the prospect of visiting Morocco and learning more about the opportunity being offered to him. He accepted the invitation without hesitation, and before returning to his own country, arranged his visit to Morocco within the next few days.

The flight to Rabat from London, took four hours. Simon was met at the airport by a senior government official standing at the foot of the steps of the Air Maroc 747. He was being given Moroccan hospitality usually reserved for a very important person.

'Very glad to meet you, Monsieur Duval,' said the official welcomingly in perfect English, but with a slightly French accent. 'I have heard so much about your wonderful achievement with the Earth Museum in London, and have been looking forward to meeting you. Please this way...'

Bypassing all formalities, Simon and the official were ushered into a black Mercedes Benz saloon car with chauffeur standing on the tarmac, and whisked away to the seat of the government.

Situated on the Altantic coast, just north of Casablanca, Rabat was the administrative and political capital and also where the main residence of the monarch, and the foreign embassies were located. Even though Rabat is the modern capital of Morocco, it was distingished by its lack of hustle, although the people in the street appeared cosmopolitan. Much to Simon's delight, the city enjoyed a legacy of wonderful Art Deco buildings from French colonial times. The view out of the car window was a kaleidescope of architectural treasures.

All the administrative buildings appeared to lie on or off one of the main thoroughfares, where the Mercedes drew to a halt outside a modern structure with Arabic letters over the main portal.

Again all formalities were waived as they entered. The ministers of public works, internal affairs and arts and culture awaited Simon's arrival in an ornate boardroom, which displayed the Moorish origins of the décor. The minister of public works presided, bidding Simon welcome to Morocco and making him feel at home.

Over mint tea, the minister of public works presided as host. Monsieur Abdel El Houcine explained the purpose of the invitation to Simon to visit Morocco.

'From time to time, the King delegates various visionary projects to his ministers to explore and develop as an idea. However, His Majesty has asked me to tell you that he has visited the Earth Museum a number of times and was most impressed with the power of your architecture to convey the intended message to the average person. Therefore, he would like you to bring some of that genius – I use that word sincerely – to bear on the project he has in mind for the Western Sahara. You do know about the history of the Western Sahara, Monsieur Duval?'

'Yes, your ambassador, Monsieur al-Hassan in London gave me some useful insights into the history of the territory and I have done some reading. Thankyou.'

After tea a map was projected onto the wall on which various features of the territory had been charted.

'If you are agreeable we will fly with you to Laayoune later today and then on to the Dakhla peninsula?' suggested Monsieur El Houcine. Simon nodded his approval.

'It is a unique coastal finger located well within the Western Sahara. The project we are considering is destined to be developed there, however, in the meantime, let me describe in broad outline what the King and his government have in mind.'

Simon listened closely recording useful facts on his electronic notepad. The minister spoke almost confidentially.

'I suppose I have no need to tell you, Monsieur Duval, that the United Nations organised a ceasefire in 1991 with a view to a referendum being held thereafter. That situation remains on hold. Meanwhile money has been poured into the territory by Morocco to build up its infrastructure, and cities like Laayoune have expanded. With the prospect of employment many Moroccans from the north have been attracted to move there – it is a tax-free area, you can imagine the attraction, oui, Monsieur Deval?'

The monologue went on so long, Simon started wondering when the history lesson would finally get to the point.

'So far,' Monsieur continued enjoying the attention of the moment, 'all the government's efforts to upgrade and develop the territory have been channelled into rather mundane but essential infrastructural improvements. Now, the King - supported by the government - believes that the time is ripe for other human needs to be addressed – such as a world-class playground for locals and tourists to enjoy.

How would you call it - a goose that will lay the golden egg? Call this a political strategy if you like, but it is necessary, not only for the financial coffers, but to win the hearts and minds of the indigenous peoples there which can help to stabilise the territory's future.'

' A playground? thought Simon, 'now that could prove to be exciting! I must think more about which goose will lay that golden egg.'

'Now, Monsieur Duval, do you have any questions at this stage? We would rather you saw Dakhla yourself, so that you have firsthand knowledge of the place before we go into any further detail on the project. Please be assured that your ideas will be crucial to its success. Naturally, en route we shall have time to discuss and enjoy Moroccan culture with you and then, from the air, it will be possible for you to see the country as it stretches inland from the Atlantic coast. Thanks are due to the marvel of air travel, otherwise we would take many days to reach Dakhla by road!'

The cabin the departmental ministers and entourage occupied on the flight to Dakhla was a veritable living room. From the route the aircraft flew, Simon could see the occasional dry river bed, and the seemingly endless coastline. The desert simply stopped at the sea, and dropped away in sheer cliffs, leaving only a narrow strip of beach.

The hinterland to the east was stony desert from the coast to the horizon. Finally, the small town of Dakhla appeared below them, located on the end of a sandy peninsula, just north of the Tropic of Cancer. The finger of arid land ran parallel for forty kilometres down the Atlantic coast enclosing a wide waterway, the only physical relief in the long coastline, a very long away from anywhere.

The town was populated mainly by soldiers. It was known for ocean fishing, and surfing– *two potential attractions for the leisure-seekers*, noted Simon. His hosts checked the ministerial party into the town's top hotel, which was filled with United Nations personnel, but clearly government members enjoyed priority and the top floor of the building was reserved for their exclusive use.

Simon was taken on a tour of the town and the peninsula. He liked the potential he saw in Dakhla, a place as yet unsullied by the imported international culture which had begun to manifest itself in so many once exotic parts of the globe.

The town had a low-key response to its geography, a place where the wet ocean body and the dry desert collided - the extremely large wet ocean meeting the extremely large dry desert. This could provide an opportunity for distinctive architectural forms, whatever the brief was going to be.

A special function room had been laid out in the hotel for the party to hold their meeting. Simon's hosts were most attentive and he awaited for the start of the meeting with mounting enthusiasm. All discussions from now on would be recorded on videotape so that the King might have a first-hand account of the interchange of ideas.

The minister of public works opened the meeting in French and Arabic, welcoming the visiting party and the local administration officials. Simon, who spoke only English, was assisted by an interpreter. *There were about fifty high ranking people in all*, Simon guessed, so this project was high on the government agenda.

Minister Abdel El Houcine, turned to Simon:

'Monsieur Duval, again our sincere appreciation for undertaking this journey with us. We look forward to very fruitful discussions. As you can see, Dakhla due to its unique location has enormous limitations but also potential. It has harbour facilities, an airport, and road system which is a good start. No doubt these will have to be upgraded. However, as you can imagine, the lack of sufficient fresh water will place a major limitation on any future development – he pronounced 'development' as the French do - let us say that desalination of sea water is going to be a priority. I am sure all agree with that obvious conclusion.' Simon nodded.

The meeting dealt first with the extreme climatic conditions. No matter what development took place, with the hot desert winds and cold sea mists the architecture would need to respond to those challenges in order to provide a good level of comfort for the occupants.

Simon offered his initial thoughts:

'I would like to say that I see those extremes as 'positives' in terms of the kind of architecture which is needed. A unique vernacular, particular to the place, could make Dakhla a destination for those world travellers who are bored with the traditional leisure resorts. The fact that the peninsula inlet is relatively safe water with a lengthy perimeter is in my view a real plus. There is scope here for deep water and leisure craft facilities, holiday villas and hotels with conference facilities. Delegates could be flown into another world. Provided the amenities are in place, the yachting world will come here in droves. There is big money there. The diving and snorkelling fraternity will not be far behind, followed by the surfers, albeit at the lower end of the spending scale, but they also come in their numbers, once the word gets around, so to speak.'

'Just so, Monsieur Duval. What about yacht building and the peripheral supply industries?'

'Sir, I believe you have a point there. Yacht building is big business involving mega-finance. The spenders will need to be housed during their stay, and will expect top-class hotels. I assume that a casino is not permitted on the grounds of the predominant religion?" queried Simon, but knowing the answer. He added: 'There is a jetsetting club of gamblers known in the trade as high-rollers, who bring huge dollops of foreign currency wherever they go.'

'You are correct, Monsieur Duval, in that casinos are not permitted. However, that raises another issue – places of worship. Mosques, as you have seen, are everywhere even in the smallest communities in Morocco. Moslems offer prayers more than once daily, and so it is imperative that Dakhla has a mosque worthy of its status. That will be an integral and important part of the development brief. The design of a grand mosque can be done in consortium with our own architects, or even through an international competition.'

The discussion seemed to be at and end, but the Minister continued:

'Now I have to let you into a state secret – is that how you say it, Monsieur Duval? - a thought which has captured the imagination of the government is the possibility of turning Dakhla into a freeport. Apart from being able to export the phosphate, which is in abundance here, it would stimulate the regional economy and not place such a burden on the national economy. Because of its isolation, it would not be difficult to administer, but with the right infrastructure to control the import and export of goods it can be managed. This aspect would need special attention.'

Mmm, Simon relished the thought, that idea of a freeport could drive a whole lot of other ideas.

Although the buildings of Dakhla were not inspiring, being mostly a faltering mixture, which Simon labelled 'mod-moroque', exciting opportunities for a new architecture waited for him to exploit. To the meeting he suggested a presentation of a concept after three months, stressing that he would need the expertise of others, such as urban designers and civil engineers to develop it further.

'Those experts will all have to be Moroccans, Monsieur Duval - they will lay the ground plan,' said the Minister. 'I can assure you they will be only the most experienced professionals.' Simon nodded his approval.

The initial fee offered was acceptable to Simon, whether the project advanced to the next stage or not. If the project did indeed advance to the next stage, he would be offered a studio and Moroccan staff and consultants at government expense in Marrakesh, a city at the foot of the High Atlas mountains. From there he can fly direct to Dakhla and land there within an hour. Marrakesh offered an authentic mix of Moroccan culture which would be essential to his creative endeavours.

I will bring my home team with me, he considered quietly to himself, to share the creative challenge. And my good friend Nick of course as project manager.

Simon woke drowsily forgetting where he was. As he surfaced, Ingrid propped herself up and watched him in amusement, mischievously stroking his nose.

'Guttentag, meinen liebschen,' she teased in her native tongue. 'You slept like the dead.' She placed her arm across his chest, kissed him passionately on the cheek. She and Simon were now seeing one another seriously, and spending the odd night together. For any observer, it was obvious there was a deep commitment between them - wedding bells should not be far off.

'I dreamt of a wild Arabian night with you in a Berber kasbah,' he teased. Then more soberly, 'This Moroccan project is going to take on a life of its own, and I am going to be sucked into vortex of a very demanding job. That means, Ingrid *meinen liebschen,* that you must hire a little cottage in Marrakesh when the job takes off, so that I don't fret about any other man you might be dating behind my back – and you can look after my washing and ironing.' Grinning, he waited for her reaction.

'Morocco has wonderful gemstones which make great jewellery – perhaps you could bribe me, but not to wash and iron for you, Herr Simon Duval,' she quipped. He loved her quickwitted responses to his teasing.

They parted at Frankfurt airport, from where, for the time being, Simon would return home to apply his mind to the Dakhla challenge. Although he is to be away from Ingrid for three months, he was looking forward to being with his crack team in deep south on African soil.

In the Cape Town office, the team had waited impatiently Simon's return as, in the interim, maps and other information had been couriered by the Moroccan ministry of public works. He took them by surprise and swept in like a summer breeze. It all looked so exciting and they were keen to put on their creative caps. A vast table top had been installed to spread out the documents sent for the project. The site was enormous, with so many options and opportunities that it was difficult to know where the project started and where it ended.

Simon suggested they first review the state of the existing infrastructure, climate, ecological sensitivity, transportation and above all water. The latter was key to the success of the freeport.

To foresee how the architecture would evolve stylistically was probably the most difficult at this stage. It seems that most materials would have to be shipped by sea to the site, a constraint which could be helpful in steering their creative ideas about building design. The team settled down with mugs of coffee and listened in rapt attention to Simon's descriptions of Moroccan culture and the challenge of the new Dakhla Freeport.

As he talked the ideas began to take shape: 'There is no "sense of place" nor romance about present-day Dakhla – it is pretty banal, but the opportunity it offers is mindblowing,' reported Simon. 'It needs a massive architectural landmark to help it out of its identity crisis, and I have been thinking of a gigantic gateway, or portal, through which container vessels and yachts could pass into quieter waters and where wharfside architecture would be located - not to forget a huge housing component for the wealthy and the workers.'

The concept of a giant portal grew more convincing in Simon's mind.

'Imagine,' he continued, 'across the narrower end of the sea inlet a huge arch, contructed in steel with a tilting bridge below to allow for ships and seagoing yachts to pass through. You know like the famous London bridge. The two halves would each suspended from a huge iconic Moorish arch - you know - curved like an onion and climaxing to a point at the top. For added interest, the two halves – one from the Atlantic side and the other from the desert might just not quite meet at the top. I estimate the arch being located about here,' he said, using a pointer on the map, 'which means that with its approaches from either end, the bridge could end up being one kilometre long!'

'Yes, and maybe the arch and bridge could be of spaceframe construction, so that the Moorish opening could look as though it had been cut out of a mesh of triangulated tubing?' said Rollo.

'Good thinking,' Simon replied. Rising to the growing enthusiasm for the concept, he suddenly saw another dimension - how this groundbreaking project could symbolise the New Age in a world wrestling with strife and tensions.

'Why don't we name the World Friendship Freeport -or just the Friendship Freeport? I'll suggest that to the Moroccans!'

Over the weeks that followed and as the design progressed out of the ideas from their daily sessions around the table, so a new Dakhla began to emerge from its current identity crisis. Being a freeport, the arch and the bridge would physically define the enclosure of a container terminal – and a customs control point. The Moroccans would probably find such facilities advantageous in dealing with the inevitable contraband.

For a three whole months the team committed themselves to the project, without concern about the late hours it demanded. It had indeed 'taken on a life of its own', as Simon predicted at the outset, and a new architecture was emerging with each prototype they explored – housing, warehousing, workshops, hotels and recreational facilities. The extremes of the climate were legible in their architectural solutions, and so too are the culturally familiar design elements to which Morocco faithfully returned in all their major developments. Finally, almost three months to the day, the sketch plans with a small scale model on a very large table were ready for Simon's presentation.

With three months of work to show the Moroccan ministers, Simon's concepts for the Dakhla freeport project were due for presentation to a special joint sitting of the Moroccan parliament in the grounds of the Royal palace in Rabat. The Moroccans were generous hosts and all his needs had been provided for in anticipation of his milestone presentation. He was given a suite at the top hotel on the Place Sidi Makhlouf, where he and his team were accommodated in the height of luxury. Expecting a host of technical questions, Simon had seconded Nick who by then had an intimate knowledge of the concept. Rollo was also there as general dogs-body to take delivery and look after the presentation model and drawings.

An hour before the presentation a black Mercedes Benz stretch limo, with the Royal ensign fluttering over the chrome up front, arrived to pick them up.. They were swept through the streets and entered the 'Gate of the Winds' of the Palace complex and arrived at the venue, a modern addition especially built for conferences of national importance.

A hushed silence greeted them as they entered the hall filled with an august gathering - it was as if those present were holding their breath for some extraordinary event. After the usual formalities for a joint sitting, and Simon's introduction, he was shown to the rostrum to present his concept. His nervousness was untypical, even though by now he had experience and attained considerable status as an internationally renowned architect. Here, another kind of dyamic interaction was needed as the situation required communication across a language barrier. He spoke no French, and those gathered were presumably only familiar with Arabic or French. The hall was fitted out like a mini-UN Assembly. The sight of interpreters sitting behind glass on the perimeter made him relax.

'May I introduce the concept to the honourable ministers as the Friendship Freeport!' he commenced.

Simon found his metier, and got lost in himself as he poured out the ideas. They were breathtaking in their scope and the honourable ministers were in awe. It took and hour to complete the presentation but due to the lucid graphics and the three-dimensional qualities of the model, the concept received a smooth passage and was followed by applause.

The presiding minister took to the floor.

'Mr Duval, your proposal is awe-inspiring in its scopea and I'm sure that the Rabat government will give it the consideration it deserves. At this juncture I need to explain...various splinter guerilla groups of the Popular Front in Western Sahara which have resisted any initiatives from Rabat historically, continue to be a threat to the progress of this project. The Moroccan government with the explicit approal of the King, is committed to proceed on the grounds that the Friendship Freeport could be part of the solution to the political problems of the south. And, its message to the world in general would also be profound. Here, as you have so convincingly argued, is a gesture towards opening trade to the benefit of all nations. At the same time, it would be a masterstroke of international diplomacy, and would help to resolve the latent Western Sahara tensions.

The Moroccan government, with the explicit approval of the King, eventually resolved to proceed on the grounds that the Friendship Freeport was part of a solution to the political problems of south.

As had been agreed with the ministry, Simon's office moved to Marrakesh. His team, Rollo, George and Stefan from back home joined him in his studio within the walls of the historic medina. They were all housed in a vast, spacious apartment on the second floor. Having secured the appointment as project manager for Simon's portfolio of the Dakhla work, Nick had been allocated a small office adjoining.

Two years passed with such rapidity that Simon lost count. The project was mammoth in scale and demanded almost all his waking hours.

His master plan for the project had been adopted in its entirety and he had secured the lion's share of the architectural work. For the entire first phase, which included the new Dakhla hotel and conference facilities, the wharfside stores and workshops, the government had commissioned Simon as the architect.

Ingrid joined him for short visits realising that staying too long with him in Marrakesh distracted him.

On one of his regular visits, he landed in Dakhla after a flight from Marrakesh. The groundwork was well underway. From the air the impact of the massive earthmoving equipment could be seen, reshaping the contours of the peninsula and coastline for the new harbour and its wharves. Engineers had faithfully interpreted his design for the vast iconic Moorish arch in a neat steel spaceframe, rising impressively to one hundred metres towards the apex with its silvered, shimmering in the sunshine. Steelworkers at the top receive a continual stream of steel components which were then welded into place. Already with its distinctive form it was beginning to establish Dakhla's new identity on the international map.

The tllting bridge spanning across the waterway at the base of this enormous portal was already completed to ease the flow of traffic from the mainland to the peninsula. Most of the materials arrive by sea, and are transferred to lighters which steered their course up the inlet, making their deliveries at the newly constructed wharfs.

Hundreds of construction workers were housed either in camps or in boats moored offshore. There was comfort in the thought that the energy and resources being spent on this project could only add value and promote the success of the new harbour as a freeport. With its brand new world class facilities, its future as a recreational resort of international note would also be assured..

The view from the top of steel Moorish arch was breathtaking. Simon, with Nick and the engineer, Achmed, were lifted by crane in a bucket to the highest point. A bird's eye view of the project showed the Dakhla peninsula being transformed from a 'nowhere place' into a new port of entry into southern Morocco.

One of the workmen broke from the rest of his team nearby and approached Simon. He appeared agitated and interrupted their conversation, while pointing to a large white car way down below. He spoke with some urgency in broken English:

'Monsieur, that important man wants to speak with you - you to come as soon as possible – please, this way.'

Simon looked at the others and shrugged. He gestured

to the crane driver to lift him down and was met on the ground by a man dressed all in blue like the Moors of the south. 'This way please,' he said politely but with some determination, ushering Simon towards the waiting car.

As the rear door opened, he noted that the darkened glass windows revealed nothing about the occupants. He stooped to peer into the dark interior then felt a strong hand shoving him firmly inside and shutting the car door behind him.

'What the hell is going on?' he questioned, looking around at three other occupants. He felt for the door handle but the doors were centrally locked.

'Mr Duval, please don't worry, you will not be harmed,' said a portly individual sitting on the rear seat.

There was a lively exchange between the three occupants as the car sped off with a roar in the direction of the desert. Simon was unable to elicit any information from any of his abductors. Clearly, though, they had some connection with a reactionary group, and he was being used as a political pawn. Across what seemed to be uncharted desert, the car was driven expertly with the driver picking out tracks not legible to the untrained eye.

The landscape was parched and sandy and whatever vegetation there was to be seen, survived only by the moisture that moved in from the ocean at night. The occupants conversed little but always in Arabic. It seemed to Simon that there was some disagreement about the fact that now that he was in their custody, their situation had become more earnest. The word 'Americaine' came up indistinctly in their conversation. Simon's questions drew curt responses from the portly one, who spoke English with a strong accent.

It was dusk before the driver slowed the vehicle over a rise. Through the darkened glass car windows Simon could see a Bedouin camp near an oasis, a short distance away. Before leaving the vehicle, his hands were bound in front of him - being tied in front seemed to imply that he was being treated with at least some respect. With his eyes blindfolded they left the car and trudged in the direction of the camp where they were met by a contingent of turbanned figures chattering unintelligibly.

His hands were untied and the blindfold removed in a tent. He was told to change out of his western clothes and then to don the dress of the desert people – a jellaba and turban. *This was not going to be believed back home*, he was able to find the situation amusing as he stalked around testing the effect of his foreign attire. He took stock of his surprisingly luxurious cage – a tent of thick woven camel hair, noticably warmer inside despite the evening cold.

Layered on the floor were woven carpets of a high quality with large scatter cushions and low decorated furniture standing around the perimeter. He drank water poured from a ceramic jug, and ate fruit from a bowl. *Clearly, they were giving him the soft treatment, but what was this all about? No doubt he would soon find out.* He re-arranged the cushions and lay down waiting for some hint of what was in store. Nothing came, other than a meal of a *harira*, a soup with lentils, brought and served by a member of the camp who remained silent throughout. The night was spent fitfully in his unfamiliar captive state.

The following day, each of his three captors came in turn to inform him of a meeting with the 'important' person, descendent of a once ruling family. Mid-morning he was again blindfolded and led from his tent across the sands to another tent, where there was a short exchange. A hand lowered his head so that he could enter through a low, curtained opening. Inside, his blindfold removed, Simon saw the enormous interior of the tent, lavishly furnished as if it were a permanent structure.

All those present were standing reverently awaiting the arrival of someone who would probably turn out to be their leader. After some minutes a man with a small entourage entered. His manner and bearing seem to indicate that his title was secure by the laws of inheritance. With the help of his two headmen he settled himself crosslegged onto a low seat. There was some whispering with his two headmen before he looked up and stared long and hard at Simon, and, as if for a photograph, he grinned widely showing a mouth full of gold teeth.

'Monsieur Simon Duval, I must offer my apologies for your appalling treatment by my people. We are in fact gentle people, not wanting to cause injury to anyone. I am known amongst our people as the 'caid', which means 'chief' in our culture. In any event, you will not know my real identity, as the world out there is hostile to our cause for the freedom of the Western Sahara, and there could be repercussions. Next to me are my wise men; they are my left brain and right brain when it comes to making important decisions. I have no doubt that you are keen to know why you are here, yes? But first, please make yourself comfortable in the manner of our custom.' With that Simon was shown a low chair on which to sit with legs folded.

He seized the moment with a grim expression: 'Well, Mr Caid, it did not escape me that I was taken without my permission, bundled into a car without explanation, driven for hours across the desert to an isolated camp and forced to dress in clothing which is foreign to my culture. There had better be a very acceptable explanation to that kind of treatment, sir.'

'I apologise first for the need to dress like us, Monsieur Duval. You see, you have been abducted and, for the time being, must merge with the other members of the camp.' There was a low mumble of agreement and nodding turbaned heads from the entourage. 'You are safe here, Mr Duval. The American ambassador is a good friend and supports our cause. He is aware of our – let us say strategy'.

The caid went on. 'We have taken you hostage to demonstrate our extreme displeasure with the government of the north, for proceeding with a project in our region without consultation with us, the indigenous people. Your disappearance will rouse international interest, Monsieur Duval, as you are a foreign national and force the powers to the negotiating table. As we are not given to sabotage, and cannot reverse the progress of the Dakhla Freeport, we are asking a ransom of one hundred million US dollars for your release as well as our rightful role in the region. We trust that a penalty of that amount will finally teach the government of the north a lesson. But aside from the ransom, the political role we seek in the Western Sahara, will ensure that the future economic boost which the freeport will bring, filters through to the region and not all end up in the coffers of Rabat. Does that not seem to be a reasonable request?'

'I would rather not be the victim of the politics of your country, Mr Caid. I do know that I am being used as a pawn, which in my country is a criminal act and punishable by law. I would like to be released and returned to Dakhla without delay.'

'That is not possible, monsieur Duval. Your absence from the project will – how should we say – create a crisis, as your role is pivotal to the smoothrunning of the project? We stand a better chance of our demands being noticed while you, with your major role in the shaping of Dakhla, are simply absent from the project. We will speak some more at a more opportune time. Meanwhile my people will make your stay as comfortable as possible. Good day to you.'

'A moment please, sir,' Simon said urgently, 'Am I to understand that America, through that country's ambassador, is in solidarity with your cause? What could possibly be America's interest be in the Western Sahara?'

'Ah, I was waiting for that question,' the caid said smiling, displaying his mouth of gold teeth, 'America is interested in our phosphates, which, given that enormous market, we could achieve economic independence we so dearly want. Then we could secede from Rabat control, and form our own government.

'The American ambassador, Mr Quaid, is the conduit through which we are being funded. That all ties in with our interest in the Freeport, which is on our shores with the Atlantic, with the world. That is all I am prepared to tell you.'

The caid was helped to his feet. With that all rose again and left the tent. Simon caught his breath - the coincidence was too improbable to believe - yet it was possible that Catherine's father had been part of this scheme to hold him hostage.

Simon was made to stand and again blindfolded before being led back to his quarters. He was offered books and no end of food to break the boredom of his capture – little consolation, he reasoned, considering the potential for abuse by his captors if the Rabat government didn't cooperate with their demands. But the information about American involvement and role of ambassador Quaid, preoccupied his mind rather then his possible fate.

Was there a link with his abduction, starting with Catherine Quaid, who could be masterminding a conspiracy to either emasculate him professionally or a more sinister plot to eliminate him?

Simon's sudden disappearance started an immediate official investigation. It was not long before word of his abduction was circulated in Dakhla and the news of a ransom demand from the Popular Front was received. One hundred million US dollars in exchange for his life added to the shock of those who understood the consequences if Rabat refused to cooperate.

As the abduction had been expertly carried out, speculation was rife about a conspiracy between the perpetrators and their sympathisers working on the construction site.

Nick and the engineer who were with Simon at the time he was called away to the waiting car, were not able to find the workman who had been the front man and brought him the message. The site was milling with workers - to them all look similar in their overalls. Above all, there was talk that the Americans were somehow involved with the Popular Front, a relationship which rested on that country's interest in the phosphate-rich Western Sahara. The manner of his disappearance and where he was being held roused much suspicion of exactly who were all involved.

Ingrid took a flight from Frankfurt to Marrakesh where Nick would joined her on a connecting flight to Dakhla.

She was understandably distraught about Simon's disappearance and found little comfort in Nick's version of how he had been tricked into the trap – the dark windowed car with its unknown occupants.

They decided to allow the situation to develop for a few days, to see what steps the authorities would take for Simon's release. Little did they realise that it will be a floor-pacing two weeks before the government announced its decision to the abductor's demands for proper regional representation in the Freeport project, but rejected the payment of the ransom money. The horrifying thought continually invaded their minds that Simon's life is on the line.

Nick's construction team included his own countrymen under contract, a close-knit group of devout Moslems from the Cape whose skills are essential to the high standard demanded of the job. They mingled daily with the local workers, and usually had the inside track on developments surrounding the Simon Duval abduction case. The urgency of the situation was not lost on them and Nick was handed a message with the name of the worker who approached Simon. Their description of him matched the man that Nick remembered, only because of the scar on the side of his face.

With the information to hand, and with the aid of the police, Mbari, a lowly labourer was brought in for questioning, and on seeing Nick became wide-eyed and agitated.

He revealed that he was indeed part of the Popular Front on the construction site. They were detailed to provide information to a rebel guerilla group, headed by a caid. He broke down under questioning, revealing the location of a desert camp where Simon was probably being held, but he was unable to offer more. His weathered features showed relief when told that for his own protection he was to be the first prisoner in Dakhla's newly completed high security prison.

Finally, responding with impressive speed to this new lead, a light fixed-wing aircraft piloted by the security police set out from Laayoune, to search the vast openness of the Western Sahara desert.

They followed Mbari's vague directions, but without proper GPS coordinates it was like looking for the proverbial needle in a haystack. Only a lucky break would assist their task, as the sand in the hourglass began to flow ominously. In desperation, Nick and Ingrid wanted to hire another aircraft with a pilot so that they could also assist in the search and double the chance of finding Simon. From Nick's office desk in Dakhla they telephoned the all aircraft hire companies in Layoune and Agadir to hire a helicopter, but without success. Their anxiety grew with the passage of the hours.

For an interminable time there was little word from the official search aircraft, then the shortband radio in Nick's office crackled to life. It announced that a Bedouin camp had been sighted, one hundred kilometres due east of Dakhla. The location was the oasis, Bir Anzarane. The pilot reported friendly waves from those on the ground, and no sign of any mischief.

The Laayoune airbase was advised about the impossible landing conditions: there is no way that a fixed-wing aircraft can land successfully in the soft desert sand - instead a helicopter was commissioned to fetch Nick and Ingrid waiting anxiously in Dakhla, with a view to landing at the site of the camp.

At the sound of the helicopter's approach, Nick and Ingrid sprang into action, donned their gear and headed out to the landing pad. The presence of its metal body in the early morning light became their ship of hope. The rotors kept turning as they embarked, then pilot lifted the craft effortlessly into the air. With a tilt, he swung the nose of the aircraft around eastwards in the direction of the desert. There were tears of anxiety in Ingrid's eyes, but also of resolve, as she peered into the glare of the rising sun.

The helicopter reached the Bir Anzarane oasis, swooping low over the palm trees. There was no sign of the reported tented camp, but there was a maze of tracks in the sand around the waterhole, also a single blue flag - probably left by one of the caravanserais - flapping forlornly in the ground thermals, otherwise there was nothing of any consequence. *This can't be the place or can it?* wondered Nick. Ingrid felt distinctly ill at the thought that their search might yet prove in vain.

'Please follow those tracks going north.' Nick shouted above the noise of the rotors. Nodding, the pilot dipped the craft's nose down like a bloodhound following a scent in the direction of the tracks in the sand. Before long they were hovering over a small procession of camels with blue-turbanned riders, who waved to them. There was no sign of a foreigner amongst them. They appeared to be nomads who travel light without the paraphenalia of the usual Bedouin camp gear.

The search was called off when the fuel tanks registered low. If they continued there would be insufficient fuel for the return trip to Dakhla. Ingrid was devastated by their lack of success. She leant her head back on the seat and closed her eyes as if to shut out the moment of frustration.

Communicating back to the base in Laayoune, the pilot reported the oasis clear of any habitation, despite the earlier sighting by the aircraft. Simon's whereabouts remained a mystery. The lone blue flag was all that they were able to report.

Three more days passed and the continual helicopter forays from Laayoune revealed nothing more about the mysterious desert camp, nor Simon's whereabouts. The longer Simon remained in custody, the less chance he would have of surviving, was what preoccupied her mind. Curiously, since the first ransom demand, there had been no further contact with the abductors. This could mean one of two things: that Simon had been released in the desert to fend for himself and could die, or that he had succumbed to their evil deeds and been killed.

The silence was broken by a prime time BBC news report of the Simon's disappearance and the ransom demand. The story cited the present day political status of the Western Sahara and the jockeying for control by colonialist governments in the past, culminating in the Green March which consolidated Morocco's governance of the area.

In a prerecorded message, a spokesman for the abductors appeared on the television screen against a background of the vast emptiness of the Sahara. Simon Duval would remain in custody until the ransom money had been paid, he said stonefacedly. He continued: it was not enough for his people to have a stake in the Dakhla project, but the deal included the ransom money to be paid into a Swiss bank, and that was that.

Watching the news report Ingrid's curiosity was further aroused: on the screen and in the background against the ochre sands of the desert she could make out the blue flag, flapping just as they had seen it. She pointed to the screen and the lone flag which confirmed that were was a link with the Bir Anzarane oasis, where Simon's abductors must have held him.

Ingrid yearned for a place where she could be alone, away from the bustle and activity on the site. The long unrelieved coastline seaward with its crashing surf offered the ideal place to lose oneself in contemplation. She looked blankly along the unrelieved beach in either direction. Survey flags, spaced fifty metres apart and standing as lonely markers along the shoreline, were part of the Dakhla project. Half consciously, Ingrid fixed her mind on a flimsy association connected with the flags. Then, in a flash the link became clear.

She lingered a while then stood up, arguing mentally with her own intuition. She broke into her own thoughts: *'That's it'* she exclaimed: the blue flag at the Bir Anzarane oasis - it too was a marker! Then she reasoned: *the flag in the desert is not just left there by mistake, but on purpose!*

It was a long way back to Nick's office but she had to share her inspiration. Nick immediately saw the possible link that the flag at the oasis was a marker which might tell them of Simon's whereabouts. It was a possibility they dare not ignore. *Was it too much to hope that his captors had left a message and been humane after all?*

There was a tenuous possibility but another visit to the oasis might provide a clue as to his whereabouts. Although already after dark, Nick again contacted the police in Laayoune, who confirmed that their air search had been called off. For it to continue the only option was to charter the police helicopter, which could arrive in Dakhla in the morning. Their own private search was their only chance, to solve the mystery.

Simon shifted around in the confined space of the box. The only air supply was a hole in the ceiling through which a shaft of light penetrated. At noon a vertical beam into the space made a pool of light on the floor. He had lost count of the days and had time to reflect on his fate.

The first day was probably the worst when, in the dead of night, he was woken with a lot of shouting and was hustled blindfolded out of his tent. His captors then made him climb through a trapdoor and down a ladder. They untied his hands and told him to sit down, leaving with him a guerba - a waterbag made from the skin of a goat - and some dried figs, sesame bread and dried fish kebabs. They had closed the top of his prison, a box with its sides and roof made of crude wooden planks. There were no windows, only a vent pipe.

After all the shouting in the camp suddenly came to an end, he figured that the intense silence meant that his prison was underground. He could now only speculate about what was likely to happen next. If he put his ear to the vent pipe, he could still hear shouting. His captors seemed to be in a hurry to break camp. *What was to become of him, imprisoned underground without anyone having the slightest idea of his predicament?*

The stench of stale goats milk pervaded his subterranean prison like another presence, but in time he grew accustomed to its nauseating pervasiveness. He concluded that his prison was the nomads' underground food store. In the hot climate of the desert it would be logical to store food where the temperature would remain reasonably constant - underground. In fact, he realised, his survival also depended on the protection it provided. The hours passed interminably. With his nails he scratched the number of days of his confinement on the wooden sides of his gaol - the figure seven. *My lucky number*, he mused, and he began to sing, 'It's a lovely day today, ...' but the effort in the stale stuffiness of the confined space was exhausting.

At daybreak, the Nick and Ingrid's chartered helicopter touched down on the newly completed helipad in Dakhla. They boarded quickly and the pilot wasted no time in heading the craft off to the Bir Anzarane oasis. To avoid flying into the glare of the morning light, he chose to fly first in a southeasterly direction.

When they reached the oasis they strained to see if the blue flag was still there - it was indeed. This time the pilot let the craft down lightly on to the sand but was unable to avoid storm of sand from the rotor which engulfed Nick and Ingrid as they disembarked. They trudged through the soft sand towards the flag, wondering what this lonely flag in a vast desert landscape could tell them about Simon's whereabouts. After the television interview with the spokesman, all they allowed themselves to believe was that Simon had been brought to this oasis after his abduction. There was nothing more to go on.

Ingrid approached the flag which she noticed was tied to a tubular post. A sixth sense urged her to feel into the tube with her hand for a message. She withdrew it quickly it as though she had felt a shock. Looking at Nick, she pointed to the opening of the tube and whispered urgently: 'I think Simon is down there, buried under the sand – come and listen here.'

Sure enough, Nick could hear Simon's almost inaudible voice mumbling: '¼ the trapdoor, open the trapdoor.' Nick began to dig with his hands, finally revealing the top of a wooden box - Simon's prison below the ground. They combined their efforts and dug vigorously with both hands, clearing the top of the box of the thick layer of sand. Freed of its sand covering a trapdoor seemed to rise up of its own accord as it was thrown aside by Simon from below. It took both of them to pull the trapdoor away and to help him out of his cramped prison cell.

Coughing and spluttering from the sand, he managed a grin. 'We've got to stop meeting like this!' he managed to say - just like the old Simon, never say die. His face and hair were layered with a texture of sand through which they saw only a set of white teeth and the whites of his eyes, like a comical mask. He was weak from lack of oxygen, and Nick broke his fall as he stumbled forward. Between them they helped him into the waiting helicopter.

Back at Dakhla, clutching Ingrid's with one hand and a mug of strong coffee in the other, Simon recounted his story of his capture to the police. His abductors had grown more threatening the longer their ransom demands weren't met, he told them. He had feared for his life when the aircraft flew overhead and the nomads realised their camp had been discovered. He related how they had wasted no time in breaking up into smaller caravans and planned to head off in opposite directions to defy their pursuers.

Nick shared his conclusion with them: 'The Laayoune helicopters, on the first recce, saw only one of the caravans, the others went elsewhere. They knew that dispersal is a good survival strategy.'

Simon continued his story: There had been much discussion about what to do with their captive. Their ransom scheme hadn't succeeded, but they didn't want murder on their hands. After their camp had been detected, their only option was to leave him at the oasis. Their solution was to draw attention with a visible marker, the blue flag, where he could be found. Burying him in the box was probably the most humane solution they could have devised, as the sand would have insulated the box from the extremes temperatures of the desert, hot and cold. In fact it was a cool chamber serving as a pantry for their foodstuffs.

'I got used to the smell of goat's cheese, but they could have provided me with more air and some reading matter,' said Simon sourly. He had to acknowledge that they did say they would return when the situation permitted.

He then told them about the American interests in the Western Sahara, and about the American ambassador Quaid's name being used by the caid. A strange thing, he noted, that every project he had been involved with there was the sinister presence of either Catherine Quaid or her father in whatever form. It was like being stalked, and there was a kind of pathological interest in his welfare, perhaps even his success as an architect he argued.

Nick had also picked up some clues about American interests in the phosphate deposits of the Western Sahara.

'The Americans,' he said, recalling slowly what he had heard, 'are concerned about the environmental problems of phosphate handling in the US, and are looking to Morocco as an off-shore source for the product without having to manage the impacts. So, the idea is to source the product from Morocco where the environmental laws were less strict.'

He went on, 'The Americans will support Western Saharan independence in return for the right to mine phosphates, and the environmental problems would be left for the Moroccans to solve. Of course Rabat has known of this cosy relationship for some time, and the Freeport was its response.' Clearly, there was no intention by Rabat of allowing the Americans to rape the resources of the Western Sahara and so underhanded dealings were going on. Ambassador Quaid was the cat's paw - perhaps in more ways than one!'

When news broke about Simon's discovery, the international news agencies flocked in their hundreds to Dakhla to capture his story firsthand. He was no longer the pawn in a political spat, but the hero. His face appeared in cover stories around the globe – '*Renowned architect survives an early burial*' followed by the full story.

Overnight the Moroccan government's ambitious Friendship Freeport project was brought to the notice of international investors, which created a spin-off that launched the project beyond the dreams of the government in Rabat.

There was an early bustle about the living quarters in the Marrakesh medina which had been hired for the wedding party and guests.

Ingrid and her brother's wife Helga had been up before morning light, attending to a backlog of arrangements for the wedding due to start at ten o'clock. At that early hour there was no way to rouse Simon, Ulrich and Nick who had shared rather a late night before, boozing at The Green

Parrot, a popular gathering place amongst foreigners. Marrakesh, had for a long time been an exotic refuge away from the cold winters in the north.

After the trauma of the Dakhla abduction, Ingrid accepted Simon's proposal of marriage without hesitation. Why wait any longer to share their lives together while the romance of Marrakesh was perfect for their big occasion? Friends from around the globe accepted the invitation to attend and were quartered in a rambling old riad in the medina, thoughtfully restored in the style of the old architecture.

The lane in front of their riad was decked out in fairy lights, with woven carpets hung on the walls and laid on the ground. Huge floral arrangements of white roses stood in ceramic vases either side of the entrance. The ceremony was to be conducted in a community hall by a long-standing friend of the Baumgarten family, who had flown in for the occasion, and the scene was set for a resounding launch of the young couple into married life. They would ride in a donkey cart to the ceremony and after the reception leave in the cart for a destination unknown. Simon did not trust his network of mischievious friends, and so the going-way car was neatly locked away out of sight and the honeymoon plans kept secret.

Ingrid's teutonic upbringing had taught her to be punctual at all times: her own important day was certainly not going to be an exception. She looked chic in a pale pink silk dress, with a loose, matching chiffon robe. Her hair was tied back with a tiny rose cluster and her bouquet was of white roses, tied with trailing lime green ribbons. Simon on the other hand woke late, needing to be chivvied along and helped into his black suit, so as not to be late for his own wedding.

How many times had he been best man before and was never late?

The bridal couple would go to the ceremony together. Finally, to the strains of Berber music played on a guitar-like *kanza*, they departed with an entourage of family and friends trailing behind on foot. To the rhythm of a *tabala* drum, two hired water sellers in bright red and yellow traditional costume and broad-brim tasselled lead the procession. The bride and groom made a very fine looking couple –as Simon looked at Ingrid and she looked at him with love in their eyes, the general chatter was that this was to be a marriage made in heaven.

The hall as decked out in bright bunting and there were flowers everywhere. Musicians playing the distinctly Arabo-African rhythms - owing much to Berber music - kept the party on a high. Then the dancing groups did complex circle dances appropriate for weddings - usually associated with harvest rites –to wish the wedding couple fertility and abundant issue from their union. These were interrupted by speeches from friends and family, particularly Ingrid's relations, the Baumgarten clan, who had invaded Marrakesh to be at the wedding.

The honeymoon car was a Jeep which Simon had hired for a private offroad tour. They left the wedding guests partying in full swing and took the road to the High Atlas mountains, an impressive chain dividing Morocco diagonally almost down the centre.

In the orange light of evening they stopped on the Tichka Pass at its highest point to look back . The air was exhilirating after the hot dryness of Marrakesh. Further on they encountered Berber villages along the river courses, each one with its own distinctive adobe vernacular and towering mosque, perched typically above valley floors, green with intensive agriculture in the river plains.

They arrived late and drove along the Dadès river, known as the valley of the kasbahs. Simon had arranged rooms in the main Skoura kasbah, the seat of a one- time potentate, around which nestled the simple houses of the subjects in a palmaraie. They were ushered in to a large room overlooking a courtyard of green planting where the water played gently in a fountain lined with ornate ceramics. Oil lamps bathed the rough walls with soft light. Just soaking in the ancient atmosphere of the place was romance itself.

They sat crosslegged on cushions for the evening meal, comprising traditional Moroccan cooking, the highlight being the tajine in which lamb with aromatic herbs had been prepared and served on couscous.

Simon looked at Ingrid with a grin. 'Do you remember my promise that someday I would carry you off to a kasbah? Well here we are, my love. And here's to us', he said ceremoniously. He kissed her on the cheek.

The Duvals spent the two first years of their married life in Marrakesh, loving the ambience and cosmopolitan vibrancy of the place. They adopted many of the ways of the locals, and both became fluent in Arabic. The Dakhla project took up all of Simon's working life, and after a year of working together he reluctantly allowed his young crack team to return to their home country. It was their choice after all. As a consolation to himself, he promised that he would stay in contact – perhaps they would work together again once he and Ingrid returned after the Dakhla project was completed.

He, himself, admitted to a growing homesickness as the months went by.

The date for the official launch of the Friendship Freeport arrived with a fanfare of international publicity. Hundreds of invited guests reached Dakhla either by air or sea, and were accommodated in the newly completed beachfront hotels. Royalty mixed with film stars and pop singers, who were to entertain the gathering after the official part of the function was over. Ocean-going yachts crowded the marinas and there was a Continental atmosphere in the quayside restaurants and bistros.

The Moorish arch in its complete state was a magnificent portal rising high over the waterway. It's shape had become associated with the Freeport, and, around the seafaring world it was recognised as the port's icon - all the Freeport's publicity brochures carried its image as well as the letterhead of the port authority. Many acknowledged that the design of Moorish arch was inspired, and the architect often complimented on a stroke of genius in its conception.

At the inauguration, the tilting bridge below the portal was lowered to become the centre stage for the dignitaries who were able to look down onto huge floating pontoons where over five hundred of the specially invited guests were seated.

With perfect weather that day and a calm sea, the signs were auspicious for the success of the Friendship Freeport. Motor boats brought guests to the pontoon to take their seats and buzzed back and forth from the wharfside, where the uninvited onlookers were randomly gathering. Simon and Ingrid were amongst the guests of honour on the bridge.

Following fanfare of trumpets and a roll of drums, the master of ceremonies announced to prolonged applause:

'Monsieurs et Mesdames, on behalf of the king, welcome to the new Dakhla, Morocco. His royal highness has asked me to officiate on his behalf as, regrettably, he is unable to be here on this very, very special occasion. However, he will be meeting with some of you in Rabat tomorrow at the royal banquet.'

The ceremony took the usual route of awarding credits to all involved in the Friendship Freeport, referring often to the architect, Mr Simon Duval, who was ushered to the rostrum to share with the gathering his vision for the design. At the end he received a standing ovation. The media photographed the gathering of dignitaries extensively while the television cameras were cosily ensconced in the structure of the Moorish arch, beaming out their images to the networks.

From below, the view looking up to the arched structure was awesome with its opening cut-out like the ubiquitous Moorish arch as Simon had promised. It was decorated with colourful banners for the occasion and symbolised an opening to a new world for Dakhla – and a fitting portal into Morocco from the south – from which the whole country would benefit.

A flypast of jet fighters marked the sky overhead with colourful trails, heralding the celebratory part of the programme. To the sound of marching music a procession of camels and their drivers started to move into view followed by decorated carts and floats, Bedouin dancers, the 'blue' people of the south, and groups representing the whole of Morocco in their traditional dress. The procession entered the bridge from the east bank and progressed noisily and colourfully across in front of the seated dignitaries. At the same time, spouts of coloured smoke to match the national flag of Morocco poured from the top of the Moorish arch into the bluest of blue skies.

Simon's eyes were wet with silent happy emotion. He was in a trance with seemingly endless handshakes being offered to compliment him on his achievement. Some well-wishers didn't hesitate, and invited him for further commissions, but his exhaustion forced him to decline all offers for the time being.

Chapter Five

Ten years later

Dr Stephens requested that Ingrid share her insight into the possible causes of Simon's condition. He chose a project which seemed to have a bearing on the Quaid's role in Simon's psychotic episodes.

'I was fortunate to have met your brother, Ulrich Baumgarten, when he was in the Cape,' Dr Stephens said, 'And he gave me some background as to the interference of the American ambassador Quaid in trying to overturn the result of the Earth Museum competition which they had won. As America was an important patron to the cost of that project, it could have gone the other way.'

'I remember, Dr Stephens, that an American architect could have been awarded the commission to ensure that the Americans didn't withdraw their contribution to the Earth Museum,' Ingrid recalled.

'Exactly. That is what Simon has told me. Catherine Quaid's father agitated and threatened to withdraw American support, just as he did with the Anglican Cathedral in the Cape. Simon and Ulrich got to hear about the behind the scenes flurry for the first time on the Michael Flanagan TV show when they were asked why their "undoubted success was marred by scandal in the corridors of power".

'That day they were both extremely upset. And, Simon had no doubt that the Quaids were angling for the job, trying to pull strings behind the scenes. He didn't then take it personally…'

'Oh, but he did, Mrs Duval, he did. After his and Catherine Quaid's paths had crossed numerous times before, he began to believe that their poisonous arrows were aimed at him. It didn't matter so much as to why they were getting at him, but rather that they were. Ulrich, your brother, was unaffected by the previous interventions into Simon's professional and personal life.'

Stephens' psychiatric experience told him that repetitive coincidences begin to take on certain meanings, sometimes good, and sometimes bad. In Simon's case the Quaid incidents were too frequent to be ignored and were settling deep into his psyche.

'To take this line of investigation further, I want you to take me on a journey to the next project which Simon, now a rising star on the global architectural scene, was commissioned for. He told me it was the one in Morocco, on the Dakhla peninsula, a phenomenally isolated peninsula on the shores of the Atlantic. I think he called it the Friendship Freeport?'

Ingrid nodded. 'That is what it was called, and it was a visionary project launched by the Moroccan government – like a friendly gesture to the world. I would be glad to share what I know with you, Dr Stephens.'

After what Ingrid had told him about Simon's experiences with the Moroccan project and his incarceration below the desert sands at the isolated Bir Anzarane oasis, where he might never have been found, Dr Stephens had more clinical evidence for understanding the main causes of Simon's plunge into psychotic delusions. The Quaid factor had brought on his retreat into himself, as a form of mental defence against their wilful hostility. He had never consciously thought that their continual resistance to his progress would seriously derail what had become a brilliant career. But it had to the makings of doing just that.

In the consulting rooms of Dr Stephens, psychiatrist, His Worship the Archbishop browsed through the medical magazines to pass the time. The doctor was running late with his patients. He sent word that the Archbishop should be offered a cup of tea.

Finally they met and the Arch was installed in a comfortable seat in the corner of the psychiatrist's panelled office. Stephens explained that Simon was under his care, and he was interviewing those with whom he had contact before his illness. He knew, he said, that the Archbishop held Simon's professional abilities in great esteem and could perhaps throw some light on the matter of Simon Duval's winning Cathedral entry, the drama which surrounded the jury's final choice of the winning design, and the hint of plagiarism by another entrant, none other than Ms Catherine Quaid.

After expressing his dismay at the news of Simon's illness, the Arch cast his mind back to the time of the competition.

'Let me explain, Dr Stephens. The rules of the competition were very clear. For the jury to be absolutely fair and objective, participants were instructed not to disclose their identities on their entries, except in a sealed envelope on which should appear only their submission numbers.'

'Therefore, it would be difficult for anyone to influence the jury?' Stephens concluded.

'Exactly. But you see, Dr Stephens, even after the best scheme had been announced, a carrot which would have assisted the church's soup kitchen project was dangled in front of the jury in an attempt to swing it's choice of the winning design. I was telephoned by the American ambassador, Mr Quaid, and asked to review the choice of winner in favour of his daughter, Catherine, so that he could recommend to the American Episcopalian church that a sizable donation to the soup kitchen project would be appropriate. It was of course tempting for the church to agree as many children and out-of-work adults living on the Cape Flats would have enjoyed the benefit of that donation. However, a bribe is a bribe, and the church cannot be party to that!'

'As I understand the situation, Your Worship.'

'Oh, yes, Madam Catherine is a chip off the old block, I would say.'

'There was also talk of plagiarism. Would you mind explaining the circumstance'.

'With the greatest of pleasure,' said the Arch.

During the second session with Ingrid Duval, Dr Stephens explained his prognosis.

'Simon has linked two people about whom he has experienced continual nightmares. He firmly believes they played a part in the unfortunate drug incident in New York. They are Catherine Quaid and a man called Pierre. Simon thinks that they connived to doctor his drinks, and to arrange for drugs to be planted in his clothing. He says he has reason to believe that Ms Quaid would like to render him a non-competitor in the architectural profession by ruining his ability to practice and destroy his public image. Does this make any sense at all Mrs Duval?'

'Indeed it does, doctor,' Ingrid said finding the link plausible. Simon had many times told her of Catherine's egotistical competitiveness, and Pierre was the host on the night that Simon ended up on a drug charge. She had decided to bide her time until he is fully recovered before exploring that likelihood with him. She had known the pressures that Simon was experiencing in the Big Apple, aggravated by being alone; above all she trusted him. Little had she expected that she would be flying to New York to bring him back home, strapped to a stretcher.

'Let me continue on a hopeful note, Mrs Duval. Simon's full recovery cannot be guaranteed. However, in time he will be able to enjoy family life and take up his profession again, under a regimen of the proper medication, plenty of exercise, no stress or strain nor long hours that could lead to fatigue. He should be seeing me at least twice every month, just to monitor his improvement and tweek the prescription that he is on.'

He continued. 'Simon says it feels as though he standing in the mist and looking down a tunnel of light with his own shadow at the far end,' Stephens explained. 'This was an experience he once had on top of a mountain, a phenomenon known as the *brockenspectre*, but this time in his shadow he thought he saw his image with angel wings and believed that he was the Archangel Gabriel.'

'Is that positive, Dr Stephens?'

'Yes, I believe it is.'

'And one other thing,' continued Stephens. 'In the New York hospital he hallucinated about imaginary creatures, these very two persons, both of whom he perceives as adversaries as I mentioned earlier. He seemed to fixate about both, who he perceived as adversaries. During particularly bad periods, a transparent cat, he recognised as Catherine, appears like a hologram at the end of his bed, and a stork, the man Pierre, with a long bill hovers over his chest. During a psychotic episode the whole experience became a terrible reality. The figures held a running conversation about their intentions: to scratch his eyes out so that he could not design again, and pluck his heart out so that he would no longer have feelings.

Dr Stephens continued: 'In the continual debate over his destiny between these figmentary creatures, he tells me he pleaded with the cat and the stork not to remove his eyes and heart, but found little sympathy. The cat would came up to his face and lick his chin, as the stork pecked at his chest. He would wrestle with the straps binding him to the bed and shout for help. Then, he said, a flapping shadow on the wall always stopped the stork and the cat in their tracks, and they would disappear. He would look up and would see the Archangel Gabriel, sitting on the window cill.

'However, that is a sign that his prognosis for full recovery is good because he showed the strength to fight back.'

Ingrid looked enquiringly at Stephens.

'Let me explain, Mrs Duval. He saw the Archangel Gabriel as his champion who fought to save him. Significantly he believed himself to be that power figure, which means that in fact he intervened to save himself. A good sign, but only a start.'

Dr Stephens proceeded to outline the next stage of his treatment..

'To complete his recovery, I want to interview all those dear to Simon so that together we can plan a way to his complete recovery. Who do you suggest we start with?'

'I think, maybe Nick, his friend and colleague, Ingrid suggested, 'They have been close since childhood, and are business partners. He is optimistic, good-humoured and straightforward – a Sagittarian, if you know what I mean…

Dr Stephens called Nick and asked him to meet with him at his rooms. He had concluded that Nick's close friendship held the key to lifting Simon out of the doldrums and putting smile back on his face…

Dr Stephens' secretary picked up the phone, and turning to Nick said, 'Dr Stephens would like to see you now, Mr Nikolaides.'

There was a relaxed air in the consulting room, and Nick shook the psychiatrist's offered hand. Jokingly, he lay down on the couch. They both laughed.

'Thank you for coming… may I call you Nick? Let us say that your lifelong friend, Simon Duval, is with us in absentia, shall we?'

Nick nodded.

During Nick's third session with Dr Stephens, he said that a court order had been served on Atlas Company to halt any further activity on their site, and he continued to report to Simon daily on the situation. Simon, he said, was shocked over the revelation that American interests were bringing pressure to bear in the corridors of power.

'Was this the first time that the name Quaid came up?' Stephens asked.

'I think so.'

'Had Simon met Catherine Quaid at that stage, either socially or professionally?'

'Not as far as I know. Things got really nasty on the Southcape site when the Atlas Company went ahead with what they called 'Plan B'. You see, progress in the construction was pleasantly smooth for weeks until the first phase of our building collapsed overnight. I was completely baffled as the structure was cellular and the walls were all raised together for lateral support.

'Simon had hoped for a clear run in the office, but building site crises often seemed to bedevil such plans. He rescheduled his day, and arrived at the site within minutes. On inspection one corner of the front house had collapsed. In the pile of broken walling we looked for evidence of construction failure, but the bricks were all well-bonded – so, Simon concluded, there was nothing wrong with the cement mix. We searched for any clues, but there were none. The foundation remained sturdy and a good base for the superstructure. The cause of the collapse was baffling.

'As if with a sixth sense, I sniffed the air, and told Simon that I smelt cordite which could mean explosives, otherwise foul play. Then, looking at the ground we saw distinct evidence of burn marks along the edge of the foundation. That could only have been caused by a fire or an explosion. It certainly wasn't bad building, causing the wall to topple. But, who would want to sabotage the construction?

'A strong wind had howled across the site on the night of the collapse and the nightwatch had reported a muffled noise. When he saw no movement he assumed all was well. We decided to get the nightwatch to move from his usual spot and keep the floodlights on as usual. We got him to call us if anything suspicious happened. We could both be at the site in ten minutes, no matter what time of day or night.'

'The security fencing was designed to be completely proof against any trespassing, and the collapsed wall was some distance from the boundary. We discounted the possibility that an explosive had been hurled over the fence. It had to be an inside job, but the nightwatch had nothing to gain by it…'

Doctor Stephens interrupted, 'I believe that if we revisit and remind Simon about his life's journey through his friends and those dear to him we can unravel the trauma which has given rise to his mental state. He is a fine architect with international acclaim, but it appears others are bent on undermining his professional life by undermining his confidence. If one can believe his own testimony, there were two people who orchestrated his plunge into his present state of mind in New York. But, one of them in particular seems to have crossed his path often and seems to have embarked on a personal vendetta against his progress in his profession – a woman whom I am sure you know: Catherine Quaid?'

'Yes, that much is indeed true. From the time of the Southcape project, then the Cape Town Cathedral competition, followed by his international commissions, the Earth Museum in London, the Friendship Freeport in Morocco and finally the Phoenix Acre in New York which he was prevented from completing. During all those projects the spectre of Catherine Quaid was present.'

'In what form?'

'Well,' Nick said thoughtfully, 'she was either in direct confrontation or through her influential connections she manipulated the situation to her advantage. You see, I believe that she has the talent, but prefers being top dog and will go to any length to be seen as such.'

'Do you mean that she has a competitive personality which consumes her?'

'Most definitely and well put, Dr Stephens. But how will it be possible to erase her from his mind? After all, Simon will always regard her as his adversary.'

'Well, that is where I want your to help in putting back the missing building blocks of his memory. If we can achieve that, he will regain his former confidence and be equipped to push the recent past aside, and get on with his life. Since you have known him since childhood and remain close to him, tell me what you know about his career, where did it begin to take off. His problems stem from his work, where his progress is being undermined.'

There wasn't much that Nick didn't know about Simon's career and the Atlas Tower in Cape Town where the spectre of the Quaids first surfaced.

'I have an assignment for you, Nick. The road to recovery for Simon is to return to the happy times in his life. He is frustrated by the slow progress and there is not much more we can do clinically except to explore other avenues.'

'Of course, I will help Simon wherever I can, Doctor. Where would you like me to start?'

'You shared a lot of fun during your growing up years...he was after all like a brother living in your family home. Go back a few decades, find some game or other which you played as boys. Let's see what effect that has on the pace of his recovery, which is going to happen, but it needs a catalyst at this stage.'

At Dr Stephen's instigation, Nick spent as much time as possible after work hours in Simon's company. Most often they played chess. He maintained a lighthearted mood and continually spoke of their youthful exploits. Nick was a seasoned observer of human nature and in a flash of inspiration suggested they return to the pond to see if it was still the same then as it was before. Simon needed no second invitation.

The Nikolaides family home was still in the same part of town next to the natural forest and the large pond where they played as boys. The old makeshift canoe of their childhood years lay rusting on the banks, overgrown with grass and filled with litter. The original owner, an old bachelor had passed on and the new owners were a family with three children, who played cops and robbers in the forest and fed the ducks on the pond. The parents were Nick's family's friends. They often spent Sundays together barbecueing on the edge of the forest, while the kids amused themselves amongst the trees.

On a Sunday, while the other adults were engrossed in conversation, and with seven willing young helpers Nick lifted over the old metal canoe he and Simon made in their youth on its side to remove the accumulation of litter. There it was, the 'Ark Royal', painted on the bows, with the skull and crossbones faded, but still visible. There was still soap in the creases of the tacked together bow and stern. *With a bit of luck the canoe can enjoy a last voyage and possibly the stage set for Simon's to experience his youthful past*, he reasoned.

Simon grinned when he saw the canoe, and the faded letters, 'Ark Royal'. The hours and hours of waterborne fun of their youth seemed like yesterday. Almost as though the years between had shrunk to minutes, they were transported back into their youthful element. Nick seized the moment: 'Simon, you tack the stern tight and I'll do the front.'

Nick, looking at the group of excited youngsters, said, 'OK, we can take a boy and a girl as crew.' A raucous jockeying to be one of the crew followed and he picked the two eldest who could swim.

'The rest can have a turn later,' he promised, seeing the disappointed faces.

'What about the soap to close up the holes?' recalled Simon. 'We haven't got any.'

'Well, now isn't that a pleasant surprise, here is some in my pocket,' Nick jested.

It was encouraging to see Simon's enthusiasm to relive their old exploits with the canoe. Ingrid and the twins and Estrella and the other offspring stood by quietly as the two grown-up boys readied themselves to launch the rusty old hull with the crew already aboard. They started by rolling up their trouser legs.

'Wait,' Nick interrupted their progress into the water, 'we've forgotten something! Crew, stand to attention. That's better. Now salute the "Ark Royal".' The next step was the easiest, pushing her out onto the open water. With the crew aboard, and seated in their original formation, Simon in front and Nick at the rear, the "Ark Royal" was paddled unsteadily out into the middle of the pond. With that the years seemed to roll away.

From the crew there were shouts of faked alarm as the water spouted through the poorly-sealed cracks and the canoe began to ship water. Screams from the onlookers on the bank encouraged them to row faster. Dead centre in the pond, the canoe sank beneath them. Over the splashing around and treading water, Nick shouted: 'Come, Simon, we can't let the old girl go down for good. Hold on and we'll drag her to the bank.'

They beached the waterlogged craft with the assistance of their youthful volunteers. Those who could swim fought to have turns. As the afternoon progressed, Simon and Nick become spectators to themselves as kids, watching their own children splash their way into childhood memories. For Simon, his return to the pond after many years was as though for the first time he felt himself - like the old Simon. Life was beginning to take on that old familiar meaning – except that deep down there lingered a story untold which had not been brought into the light.

Simon's condition was showing signs of improvement after the sessions with Dr Stephens, yet his confidence was slow to return, and his fixation on false belief was obstructing the return of his memory. Imaginary threats constantly bombarded his mind, continuing to traumatise him. Dr Stephens, adopting a direct clinical confrontation with the cause of the trauma, was gradually putting together the building blocks from his patient's past. Calling in Simon's closest friends and family members he believed would bring back his memory, build his confidence and give him back his quality of life. Ingrid had provided Stephens with a platform from which he could proceed with a better understanding of the adverse influences in Simon's life.

'Simon,' he said during their fourth session, 'I want to read to you how, when we first met, you described the way the cat and the stork threatened to kill you. Would that be OK?'

Stephens proceeded to read as Simon shook his head disbelievingly – he'd moved on from that.

'Do you really want to carry that memory around with you?'

'Of course not.'

'That is very good news,' Stephens said approvingly. 'Now I want to bring in the story of Southcape, to prove a link, however remote with someone in your professional background who you perceive as threat in your professional life. Unfortunately your personal life has also been affected.'

'I am not quite following, Dr Stephens.'

'Well, let us put it this way. There have been a number of concurrences, let us call them coincidences, when a certain influence has attempted to thwart your progress as an architect. I am referring to the intervention of adversaries high up who have sought to undermine your achievement. Let's start with the Southcape project, when you thought you were dealing with the criminal intent of your old employer, the Atlas Company. I have had a very useful chat to your good friend Nick. He has provided some interesting insights. Who had bought shares in the Atlas company? Why, foreign interests determined to force Mr Rosenberg to back down so that they could erect a high-rise building. Who was representing those opportunistic interests? Why, the American ambassador in the Cape. Who was the American ambassador's architect daughter. None other then Ms Catherine Quaid…'

'You mean…?'

'Yes, Simon. You have been unaware about how deeply you have been affected by external factors which have sought to hurt you, both in your professional capacity and, maybe with some hidden agenda, you personally. But let me advance the conjecture as to why that is important information. '

'Please do.'

'Well, the next time your path crossed that of your adversaries, was the Cathedral Competition. I have also had a useful chat to the Archbishop, who incidentally can't sing your praises enough. But that is on the side. He gave me a blow by blow account of how the competition was conducted and how the jury selected the winning scheme – your's. It was a carefully considered decision they came to and were delighted with their choice.'

'Yes, that was most gratifying,' Simon recalled being summoned to the diocesan office to receive the news of his win.

Stephens continued: 'The Arch gave me to understand that he had a call which opened up the whole question about the outcome. That call was from the American ambassador, Mr Quaid, who dangled a sum of money for the Archbishop's soup kitchen project, if the jury's decision could be reviewed – in favour of who? None other than his daughter's entry, that of Catherine Quaid. Are you beginning to see the connection?'

'I didn't know about the soup kitchen offer. But, I knew all about the plagiarised version of my scheme!' Simon's response was precisely what Dr Stephens had hoped for, a momentary recall of something which had trouble him in the past.

'Yes, I heard about the matter of her scheme being a plagiarised version of yours and how she manipulated the young man from your office to be the unwitting go-between.'

'Where is this taking us, Doctor? I mean, how will these links you have mentioned be of any use to me?'

Stephens was not nearly through with the treatment programme. He wanted more evidence of how a seemingly innocuous seed could grow and precipitate its poison into the Simon's otherwise healthy mind. Other projects Simon was involved with were international commissions, involving interaction in very taxing environment. The strain of performing successfully as an architect at international level could have made his patient more vulnerable, perhaps susceptible to anxiety attacks.

'Ingrid, your wife, tell me that her brother, Ulrich Baumgarten was the German architect with whom you carried out the commission for the Earth Museum of Natural Disasters in London.'

'Ah, Uli, my beloved brother-in-law!'

'I would like to meet him so that we can wind the clock back to when you and he first met, then collaborated on the Museum project…'

Ulrich Baumgarten's visit to the Cape to see Simon was serendipitous for Dr Stephens. Clearly, they were more than just colleagues or family, they were good friends. The partnership of Duval and Baumgarten for London's Earth Museum competition, and Simon's marriage to Ingrid, had reinforced their friendship.

It was some months before Simon Duval could once again hold a rational conversation. Back in the bosom of his beloved family, Ingrid and the twins and friends like Nick, he felt more complete, but his mind was still missing parts of his distant memory and rational linkages with his past. His dependency on prescribed medication was all that kept him reasonably sane.

The opportunities he grasped in the past had made him famous, a player on the international stage, but at a personal cost far beyond what he would have wished to pay. Deep down he was after all just a regular family man who enjoyed the simple things in life. How could he again become the person he was before he was thrust into the dark nightmare of psychosis?

Much of Simon's wake hours were spent sitting in the shade of the tree in the front of the family's townhouse. The twins were a great joy to him, and he played their childish games with them as though he was one of them. There was no letting up with the twins with their insatiable appetite for games, the rougher the better. They wasted no time in diving into the water and with splashes provoked him to join them. He chatted with friends and strangers animatedly, enjoying the social interaction as though he was the old Simon, but his sudden lapses into deep contemplation worried Ingrid. She resolved not to transfer her anxieties onto the children, or friends for that matter.

Exhausted from playing touch rugby with the kids, Simon threw himself down onto the lounger next to the pool. At that moment the young staff who had helped his climb to international fame, Rollo, George and Stefan and secretary Jo crossed the lawn and greeted him excitedly. They sat in the shade of the tree and talked about the directions their separate careers were taking. All had found good jobs after the firm closed down due to Simon's illness. He had opened many doors for them, they said, not forgetting the formative time they had spent in Marrakesh during the Dakhla project. Those years were meaningful and they were like one family, with Simon at the head. They revered him as a person as well as his skills as an architect. He in turn always valued their youthful and exuberant creativity. Together they had been a crack team, and the bond was still there, but their paths had separated and each one was content with their own career. They left in high spirits and relieved to see the Simon they knew was back.

Once again on their own, Ingrid joined Simon at the pool side. She took his hand and for a long time looked into his amber eyes and studied his well-sculpted features.

'I am so proud of you, Simon,' she said nuzzling into his neck. 'Your recovery is remarkable, and the medication is only part of it. You have a will to live and that is what makes me so proud of you. I understand more about Catherine Quaid's attempts to remove you from the profession you love. But I also know that you have the strength to put all that behind you. Let bygones be bygones, Simon, please.'

His expression saddened at the memory, but he nodded in agreement and smiled. The Past would remain in the Past. When his thoughts wandered back to that evening in the New York apartment, he felt he was strong enough to revisit the incident in his mind without a sense of anxiety or guilt. To him that episode characterised what was happening to the culture of the western world - certainly nothing for those societies to be proud of.

From the time that he and Nick revisited their happy times as youths – visiting the pond and launching the old canoe - he had refound the building blocks which had been expunged from his memory. The daylight had gradually filtered into the dark recesses of his mind.

The news in the international media was that both the Freedom Tower on the WTC site in New York and the

Phoenix Acre next door were well under construction. Simon still regretted the New York Authority's decision to reconstruct the site with a soaring pinnacle of defiance. He wrote to the Washington Post and the New York Times to present his viewpoint, and even spoken against a soaring tower in various forums - that a glass tower of a height which exceeds all other highrise structures in the world showed political myopia and insensitivity. In any event energy-guzzling glass skyscrapers were being phased out elsewhere in the world, in favour of green architecture that responded to the changing energy times. It was all too soon to try to mend the emotional hole in 2001 which the New Yorkers had experienced with a new controversial structure – the new building would be seen by the living to rise over the graves of the thousands who had succumbed. Perhaps he didn't know how resilient New Yorkers actually were.

Ingrid answered the doorbell. It was an international courier service with a tubular package for Simon which had all the markings of something important. She joined him again at the poolside while he pulled out the scroll inside and unrolled it.

He scanned the lines, and was barely able to get the words out as he read:

THE UNEP GLOBAL 500 AWARD

The United Nations Environmental Programme Global 500 Award

for commitment in furthering the aims of global resource conservation is to be awarded to

Mr Simon Duval Architect

Cape Town. South Africa.

The award is granted in respect of the architectural work of the recipient over the past decade, which addresses the changing social and environmental paradigms of the New Age.

More specifically this merit award is granted for the following:

The Earth Museum of Natural Disasters in London, England

in collaboration with U Baumgarten, architect of Stuttgart, Germany.

The Friendship Freeport, Dakhla, Morocco

and

for environmental design and resource conservation

in the

Phoenix Acre project, New York, USA.

The award is to made on World Environment Day

to be held at

The Secretariat Building, New Delhi,

to coincide with the

United Nations Information Technology Service Award to the Indian Government

for advances in the environmental field.

Simon stared at the scroll in silent disbelief, but Ingrid broke the stunned silence, whooping and dancing amongst the sprayers on the lawn. The twins stopped their games to join in the dance. Ingrid grabbed Simon and whirled around him like a maypole, until the four of them collapsed on the lawn, soaked to the skin.

'There is more,' reminded Ingrid, the first to recover her composure and returning to the scroll. 'Read it to us, Simon.'

He read on:

"At a formal sitting of the United Nations Secretariat¼ ' he skimmed through the lines...' it was resolved that the Asian headquarters of the United Nations General Assembly and Security Council would be located to address the needs of the emerging world. It was further resolved, after considerable research, that the choice was convincingly in favour of a location in Delhi.

"In view of the significant advance of the Indian subcontinent in the field of Information Technology, it was decided by a majority amongst the voting member countries, subject to final ratification of the Indian Government, that the city of New Delhi should become host city to the new Asian Office of the United Nations. For this purpose a new infrastructure of accommodation will be planned and designed to exploit the advanced electronic communications and media to meet present day global changes in social and environmental spheres and those of the foreseeable future. The financing of the new Asian quarters of the UN will be shared proportionally by the membership".

There followed the usual particulars and a request to RSVP.

'Wow!', was all the Simon can say. The concept was breathtaking in its progressiveness: 'Coming from the dowdy old UN, founded after the Second World War and gradually sinking in its obsolescent infrastructure, that really is extraordinary vision,' Simon said, smiling and sharing the moment with Ingrid.

He had progressed well, but Simon still harboured misgivings about appearing on public platforms. His confidence just re-won could be severely tested at such a formal gathering of thousands of invited VIPs.

He shared his anxiety with Ingrid, who typically, she encouraged him: 'You have to be there to get the reward you have sacrificed so much for. Besides, I think you have turned the corner, and deserve to get a pat on the back – a big international pat at that!'

The flight landed at 3 a.m. at Mumbai, and Simon and Ingrid had a four hour wait before their connecting flight to New Delhi. Even in the small hours of the morning the forecourt of the international terminal was alive with willing helpers, all intent on earning rupees for the most trivial of services. The travellers waved aside all help and made themselves comfortable in the departure lounge for internal flights to sleep away the waiting time.

New Delhi, and time-honoured Delhi, was alive with scooters, bullock carts and taxies weaving in and out in the seemingly endless bloodstream of the city. There were people everywhere with the sacred animals causing continual obstructions to the smooth flow of the traffic. The traffic islands were encampments for the very poor, and endless plumes of smoke rose from their dung fires. The pollution cast a soft acrid haze over the sun, yet it's rays still penetrated and burnt the skin.

Simon and Ingrid were met at the airport, and en route to their hotel passed by the Secretariat buildings at the top end of the Rajpath designed by British architects over a century ago. The buildings in sandstone were a legacy of the time of the Raj, and bore distinctive colonial styling inspired by Indian vernacular elements.

They drove by the India Gate, the All India War Memorial, and proceeded to the Imperial hotel, with its elegant approach through a line of tall bottle palms. The building epitomised the colonial old world caught in a time-warp in contrast to the India of today, which had become symbolically the centre of emerging Asia and recognised as such through the United Nation's decision to locate the Asian quarters of the UN there.

The day dawned for the celebration of World Environment Day on 5th June to be held in the forecourt of the Secretariat buildings. There were other dignitaries being hosted at the Imperial hotel, where, to their delight, they were re-united with the Baumgartens. Much water had flowed under their bridges since their joint project, the Earth Museum in London. Ulrich was his old self and conversation flowed like old times. In his mind Simon was putting the final missing blocks together and felt distinctly on top form.

A huge marquee straddled the road between Herbert Baker's Secretariat buildings providing the venue for over a thousand invited guests and their hosts, the United Nations General Secretary's staff. The view down the long straight Rajpath towards the India Gate on this particular morning was imposing in its visual power, and guests were seated so as to enjoy this aspect. The Indian Military band played light music with a ceremonial touch to entertain those already seated, and there were low murmurs and some applause as various royals or famous figures arrived to be shown to their seats. The international representation was impressive – a true gathering of nations united to oversee a world given to strife and tensions.

The proceedings commenced with prayers in all the world's main religions, after which the business of the day was presented.

The UN Secretary General took the rostrum and explained that the Security Council of the United Nations, had as the invitation said, decided that the UN as a body should relocate in its entirety to more effectively address the needs of the emerging world. That choice had been convincingly in favour of a location in Asia, in view of the significant advance of the Indian subcontinent in the field of Information Technology, and the city of New Delhi had been chosen to be the host city. With the assistance of the Indian government, a new grand complex would rise west of the India Gate, and it would straddle the Rajpath, symbolically becoming a portal to the future in its own right.

Various speechmakers followed, as if to hand on the baton one to the other. It was then the turn of an official from the Secretary General's office to take the stand:

'I now call the following architects to come forward to receive the UNEP Global 500 Award. In keeping with the objectives of the Award, and for their significant contribution to resource conservation through their practice of the profession of architecture, it is the Secretary General's pleasure to call upon the architects, Messieurs Simon Duval and Ulrich Baumgarten to receive the Award.'

'Furthermore', continued the Secretary General's spokesman, 'I have the pleasure of announcing a shortlist of architects selected by the United Nations Security Council who will be asked to form an international consortium. These architects will undertake the design and construction of the new United Nations headquarters which could take up to ten years to completion. It will be a challenge of some considerable magnitude, and undoubtedly one of the most prestigious ever undertaken on an international scale. I am able to reveal that amongst the selected list are these two lead architects who are receiving the United Nations' highest honour for their work, architects Simon Duval and Ulrich Baumgarten. I think they deserve a round of applause from this prestigious gathering.'

A standing ovation greeted those words. These were moments Simon would never forget, and this was the highest accolade he had ever received. With the rousing tribute ringing in his ears, Simon held his award aloft like a winning champion and looked down the length of the monumental Rajpath where his next project would rise– it was as though he was holding the past in this hands and the future was being rolled out before him.

*

Months pass and Simon was surprised to receive a large envelope couriered to him from an address unknown. He sliced open the package to find a card with a picture of Phoenix Acre in New York. It stood complete and impressive with its dignified exterior.

The card read:

Simon, darling, I couldn't resist sending this on to you, but also to let you know that I have been chosen to join the international panel of specialists monitoring the UN branch headquarters in Delhi.

At last we'll be working together, thanks to daddy!

Love,
Catherine

In the bottom right hand corner of the card was a monogram of two crossed velvet gloves with the initials 'CQ' in gold.

~ ~ ~ ~

www.ingramcontent.com/pod-product-compliance
Lightning Source LLC
Chambersburg PA
CBHW060750050426
42449CB00008B/1350